A WORD OR TWO BEFORE I GO

A Word or Two Before I Go

Essays Then and Now

Arthur Krystal

University of Virginia Press

CHARLOTTESVILLE AND LONDON

University of Virginia Press

Printed in the United States of America on acid-free paper

First published 2023

9 8 7 6 5 4 3 2 1

Library of Congress Cataloging-in-Publication Data

Names: Krystal, Arthur, author.
Title: A word or two before I go : essays then and now / Arthur Krystal.
Description: Charlottesville : University of Virginia Press, 2023.
Identifiers: LCCN 2023012234 (print) | LCCN 2023012235 (ebook) |
ISBN 9780813950624 (hardcover) | ISBN 9780813950631 (ebook)
Subjects: LCGFT: Literary criticism. | Essays.
Classification: LCC PS3611.R96 W67 2023 (print) | LCC PS3611.R96 (ebook) |
DDC 814/.6—dc23/eng/20230510
LC record available at https://lccn.loc.gov/2023012234
LC ebook record available at https://lccn.loc.gov/2023012235

CONTENTS

Author's Note, vii

Fitzgerald and the Jews, 1

Is Cultural Appropriation Ever Appropriate? 7

A Pleasure to Read You, 19

John Ashbery, the Poet of Our Clime, 28

Old News: Why We Can't Tell the Truth about Aging, 47

An Improbable Friendship, 63

Drawing America on Deadline, 76

The Tan Tarzan of Thump: Joe Louis and White America, 85

The Day Muhammad Ali Punched Me, 93

A Sentimental Education: The Books I Keep, 97

Barzun and Friend, 111

What's the Deal, Hummingbird? A Story, 129

Acknowledgments, 141

AUTHOR'S NOTE

Comes a sense of winding down. After seventy-five years of existence, existence is no less a mystery and on the whole rather less enjoyable. Walking is difficult; thinking, only slightly less so. Brain and organs receive less oxygen, and health issues outweigh other issues. Another source of astonishment: I've written nearly as many essays as my years on earth. And this seems to me, a man not given to hard work, a whole lot of essays.

So a small confession is in order. Many of them were composed not because I felt I had something important to say, but because I liked seeing my name in print and because I needed the money. Had I, as a young man, inherited fifty million dollars, would I have written even one essay? And what if I'd been 6′3″ tall and weighed 230 pounds and could run the hundred in 9.1 seconds, would I have been a writer? It's not that I think badly of my work, but I'd rather have composed great symphonies, or designed striking buildings, or written and directed a few intriguing films.

Now a larger confession: I've never regarded myself as an essayist. If you Google my name, up pops a photo of someone forty years younger and the designation "American essayist." Ask me what I do for a living and I'll acknowledge that I'm a writer. Ask me what I write about and I'll probably say "stuff," or "books," or "this 'n' that." This may sound disingenuous or even coy, but it's the truth. Why am I uncomfortable with the word "essayist"? I'm not sure. The word seems both too grand and too definitive and yet at the same time restrictive. And let's skip over the uninteresting point that what you're reading contradicts the very thing it means to assert. I'm well aware that I write essays, and yet I don't see myself as an essayist.

Perhaps it has to do with the fact that the essay nowadays, far from being Dr. Johnson's "a loose sally of the mind," has become associated with the intimacy of the memoir. Me, I'm not inclined to share the details of my life except on those rare occasions when I write about someone close to me. Like most writers I fell into essay writing by accident. When I was a teenager, I wrote poems and short stories, and later in my twenties I produced two novels and a novella (none, thank heaven, was ever published). It was reviewing books in my mid-thirties that led to longish pieces about the subjects of those books, and gradually—over twenty years—enough such pieces emerged for a book of my own.

If forced to describe what I do, I'd say that I write sentences that lead to other sentences. And when I consider what I do, I find there is something queer and disquieting about it. Why should anyone think his or her thoughts important enough to share? It's hubris, really, the belief that one has something to say that other people should know about, and unlike a poet or novelist, an essayist does not begin to work in order to explore new aesthetic terrain. No one writes an essay to transform the essay form.

There is, of course, satisfaction in writing. In fact, when the work is going well, I feel a rush—not sure if it's pleasure exactly—more like the exhilaration one feels when one's faculties are thrumming at full capacity. It may not be as concrete as smacking five fast balls in a row or sinking one three-pointer after another, but it still feels pretty good. There is also the pleasure of working with smart and considerate editors (there are a few) who help give shape to a piece whose flaws escape me.

But let's face it, my work is hardly a necessary commodity. Nor can I be sure that I have something to say that needs saying. Why continue then? Why indeed? To be blunt: ego. We usually use the term to identify a sense of self-esteem, which I think is what bothered Virginia Woolf in 1905 when she thought the essay form was becoming trivialized. She worried that people, simply because they *could* write, felt there was sufficient reason "to express one's personal peculiarities, so that under the decent veil of print one can indulge one's egoism to the full."

I like to think that my ego is not the villain here, at least not in the sense that Woolf meant. I can't speak for other people, but if I don't carve out some time to put thoughts into words (and then work those words over and over), I'm not sure I'll have thoughts worth knowing. F. Scott Fitzgerald says somewhere that he knew more about life in his books than he did in life. I feel the same, which is why I write about literature rather than what life throws my way.

Ego is obviously what drives writers, but essays need not devolve into "the amiable garrulity of the tea-table" or "pretend to an oracular and infallible nature." What Woolf required of writers was specificity, intimate knowledge, and "the cardinal virtue of sincerity." On this last score, she needn't have worried. Sincerity has never been more pronounced or prevalent. In the age of the Internet, the "I" welcomes us without a qualm into boudoir or bathroom, sharing thoughts that might have given Goebbels pause.

One can attach a theoretical apparatus to this trend—mainly the idea that absolutes in judgment are no longer considered philosophically or morally viable, since we all have an equal right to our responses to the world. And because one person's perceptions are no more valid than another person's, reality these days is more an individual matter than one of consensus. In his nice little book *The Meaning of Life* ("nice" because it could have been so much more despairing), Terry Eagleton reminds us that in an earlier age, life's meaning by and large "consisted of its function within a greater whole"; our peculiarities mattered less in defining us than did membership in the general category of human being. In fact, "the word 'individual' originally meant 'indivisible or inseparable from.'" According to Eagleton, "Homer's Odysseus seems to feel roughly this way, whereas Shakespeare's Hamlet most definitely does not." Indeed, Hamlet (who took shape around 1600) is Montaigne's immediate heir, a person who sees himself very much a person distinct from others.

Montaigne (1533–92), of course, invented the personal or familiar essay, and to my way of thinking, the line between Montaigne and contemporary practitioners has far fewer squiggles than, say, that between Leonardo and Rothko, or Shakespeare and Beckett, or Bach and Miles Davis. Montaigne came along at a moment when humanist philology and scientific skepticism began to usher in what John Donne, in 1611, termed the "new philosophy," which meant new ways of thinking about knowledge, reality, and oneself. For Donne, every man now considered himself a phoenix, "and that then can be / None of that kind, of which he is, but he." And what is the essay if not a signpost of one's distinctive self?

This doesn't necessarily mean that essays are irredeemably personal. *All* writing may be "a species of involuntary and unconscious autobiography," as Nietzsche characterized great philosophy, but there are varying degrees of exposure. And while the essay has certainly undergone various incarnations over the centuries—from Addison and Steele's periodical sallies to the belletristic appreciation of art and nature, and from the somewhat formal glances at the familiar moments of life to the aggressive intimacies of life's humiliations and outrages—in the end the essay does what it has always done, delivering thoughts and impressions in prose tepid or scorching and all temperatures in between. Distinctive voices abound—Johnson, Hazlitt, Lamb, Beerbohm, Woolf, Orwell, Baldwin, Tom Wolfe, Didion, Malcolm—but when you come right down to it, it's more a matter of bells and whistles than a radical reconfiguration of the form.*

This is where readers may wonder why they're bothering with an essay about the dubious nature of essay writing. But stick with me, I'm almost done. The essays in this volume, animated by a stupid, searching, trying-to-reason ego, were commissioned by journals and magazines usually with a prompt from their author. There are eleven in all, plus one short story that a number of readers have likened to an essay or memoir. It is neither. It is fiction plain and complicated, since fiction is obviously served by both reality and the imagination. I include it here because it has nowhere else to go. It's my first attempt at fiction in forty years and has a strictly pandemic reason for being. It *seems* to be quite sincere, but writers can't be trusted to tell the truth about themselves. If you want to know more about the author, read the essays, bearing in mind, of course, Barthes's dictum that he who writes is not he who is.

---

*A mighty long essay can be written about all the essays that have been written about the essay. Lately, two well-regarded writers have argued, respectively, that the personal essay is never strictly personal but must be viewed in a historical (hence ideological) context, and that such essays have lost their raison d'être because of the Internet and the election of Donald Trump. These are matters worth considering by someone with more time on his or her hands.

A WORD OR TWO BEFORE I GO

Fitzgerald and the Jews

People evidently liked to touch Frances Kroll Ring. As secretary and assistant to F. Scott Fitzgerald toward the end of his life, Mrs. Ring, who died on June 18, 2015, at the age of ninety-nine, might well have been the last person alive to have touched *him.* To shake her hand or look her in the eye was our last chance to commune physically with the writer who personified the Jazz Age and the Paris of the 1920s. Fitzgerald died in December 1940, and it's strange to think that until last month someone was around who had cooked and typed for him, run his errands, and cleaned up his messes. It's strange also to think that she was a nice Jewish girl from the Bronx.

Fitzgerald didn't exactly rub shoulders with many Jews. He was an Irish Catholic from St. Paul, who attended Princeton in 1913, and wrote books at a time when publishing was very much a "gentleman's game." There's no use pretending that he was enlightened when it came to race or ethnicity. In a particularly nasty 1921 letter to Edmund Wilson, he wrote, "The negroid streak creeps northward to defile the Nordic race. Already the Italians have the souls of blackamoors." Although he later backpedaled, calling his reactions "philistine, anti-socialistic, provincial and racially snobbish," he quickly segued into another preposterous stance: "I believe at last in the white man's burden. We are as far above the modern Frenchman as he is above the Negro. Even in art!"

It gets worse. According to George Jean Nathan, who, along with H. L. Mencken, founded the *Smart Set,* Fitzgerald "once aroused the wrathful indignation of colored elevator boys in a New York hotel where he was staying by confining their tips at Christmastime to fancily wrapped bottles of a well-known deodorant." Nathan offers no proof, but once read it's hard to forget. As for his feelings about Jews, they were more complicated. Although Fitzgerald met and admired Irving Thalberg, who, at twenty-six, headed up production at MGM, it's entirely possible that Frances Kroll was the first Jewish person he ever spent any time with. I cautiously exclude the Hollywood gossip columnist Sheilah Graham, who was born Lily Shiel in Leeds, England, to Ukrainian Jewish parents. Fitzgerald and Graham were an item, but she kept both her religion and her upbringing in what a journalist might term deep background.

No surprise, then, that Jews don't appear often in Fitzgerald's early work. Sure, there's the "small flat-nosed" Meyer Wolfsheim in *The Great Gatsby,* with his "tiny eyes" and "two fine growths of hair" inhabiting his nostrils, as well as "a fat Jewess, inlaid with diamonds" in "Echoes of the Jazz Age." But I have to wonder if such obvious stereotyping constituted true animus. The caricatures of Jews propagated by the Dreyfus affair around the turn of the century and by the German press in the 1930s were driven by pure hatred; Fitzgerald was simply reiterating a familiar physiognomic code. He was provincial but not malicious, and made similar attributions about various nationalities, including the Irish. "Jews lose clarity," he jotted in his "Notebooks." "They get to look like old melted candles, as if their bodies were preparing to waddle. Irish get slovenly and dirty. Anglo-Saxons get frayed and worn." Still, we have to admit that his portrayal of Wolfsheim, if not triggered by anti-Semitism, certainly emboldens it.

Fitzgerald would have thrown up his hands at this. According to Kroll, he was stung by accusations of anti-Semitism and maintained that Wolfsheim "fulfilled a function in the story and had nothing to do with race or religion." This function (or part of it), interestingly enough, is precisely what riles a reader like Ron Rosenbaum. By purposefully identifying Wolfsheim with Arnold Rothstein, the gambler who fixed the 1919 World Series, Fitzgerald makes him, in Rosenbaum's opinion, "the Jew who . . . violated the innocence and despoiled the purity of an iconic American institution." But we already knew that going in, didn't we? Anyway, there were plenty of Jewish gangsters around in the twenties, as well as Jewish boxers. Murder, Inc., was run by Jews, and the young Meyer Lansky and Dutch Schultz were carving out territory in New York when *Gatsby* was percolating in France. It was perfectly reasonable to make a mobster Jewish. The more salient fact is that Fitzgerald bought into racial and ethnic stereotypes and saw no reason to think deeply about Jews—that is, not until he found himself writing a novel about one, the very novel that would be typed up by a *maidel* from the Bronx.

Frances Kroll knocked on Fitzgerald's door in April 1939, when he was living in Encino, California, in a house that belonged to the Brooklyn-born comedic actor Edward Everett Horton (you can catch him in *Lost Horizon* and several Fred Astaire vehicles). The Krolls had moved to Los Angeles a year earlier, and Frances, then twenty-two, began looking for work. By pure chance, an employment agency sent her to Fitzgerald. Almost without preamble, he confided to Kroll that he was writing a novel about Hollywood, which had to be kept absolutely secret—just the sort of thing one reveals to a total stranger at first meeting.

Although Fitzgerald liked to pass himself off as a worldly man, he remained all his life a shaky coalition of contradictory emotions. He was shy, intense, insecure, boastful, eager to please, and eager to be the center of attention. He could behave beautifully one moment and badly the next. By the time Kroll came along, booze, pills, cigarettes, a bad diet, a heart ailment, and possibly a touch of TB had worn the veneer off the physically fit young man who had written some of the best stories about the imperishable dreams of fleeting youth.

He was also, as Kroll soon realized, a frayed alcoholic and a difficult man to work for. "Nothing was simple with Scott Fitzgerald," she recalled. "Mundane tasks became extraordinary . . . a test of nerves." Yet somehow the erratic, once-famous writer and the shy, even-tempered girl from the Bronx became friends; and one hopes that by then Fitzgerald had a better idea of where Kroll hailed from. According to Fitzgerald's biographer Matthew J. Bruccoli, Fitzgerald lived for a time, in 1919, in a small apartment on Claremont Avenue, near Columbia University, which, for some reason, he believed to be in the Bronx.

In Kroll's charming, unself-conscious memoir, *Against the Current,* Fitzgerald comes off as a polite, sickly, appreciative, middle-aged man who seems genuinely interested in Kroll and her family. Her portrait is affectionate, but not skewed. Her boss's flaws are on display, but so is a basic decency that compensated for the binge drinking and occasional foolishness. Kroll idolized him, forgave his weaknesses, attended to his needs, and when he made a half-hearted pass at her had the grace to ignore it. She became his confidante, and even acted as a mediator between Fitzgerald and Graham, whose relationship had, let us say, its ups and downs. There were "some wild exchanges between them" is how Kroll put it.

In the summer of 1939, Fitzgerald started to work in earnest on his Hollywood novel, the unfinished "The Last Tycoon," in which the hero, Monroe Stahr, is based on Irving Thalberg. Although Stahr's Jewishness is occasionally alluded to, it's never disparaged. At one point, a director gazes consideringly at Stahr and muses, "He had worked with Jews too long to believe legends that they were small with money." Elsewhere, the narrator describes Stahr enigmatically as "a rationalist who did his own reasoning without benefit of books—and had just managed to climb out of a thousand years of Jewry into the late eighteenth century." It's hard to know what Fitzgerald meant by this. Was Stahr among the few Jews capable of making the transition from the Middle Ages to the Enlightenment? In that case, the remark has a distinctly condescending flavor. And why the tail end of the Enlightenment rather than the middle? Every once in a while, you have to wonder if maybe Hemingway was right: Fitzgerald really "couldn't think."

That line aside, there's no trace of anti-Semitism in the novel. Stahr is admirable in almost every respect, and only a determined political correctivist would be bothered by another character, "a middle-aged Jew who alternately talked with nervous excitement or else crouched as if ready to spring." It might be that Fitzgerald was now compensating for his distasteful portrayal of Wolfsheim, or maybe he didn't want to be labeled anti-Semitic in an industry populated by Jews, or maybe he was mindful of what was going on in Europe in 1939. Or just maybe the fact that he spent the greater part of his days and nights with two Jewish women contributed to his portrait of Stahr.*

As Kroll tells it, Fitzgerald displayed a great deal of curiosity about Jewishness, pestering her about Jewish characteristics and customs. He was fascinated by "the Passover feast" and the practice of keeping kosher. After learning that Kroll's father had emigrated from Russia at age sixteen, he impulsively sent him a King

* It should be noted that he and Graham had a number of Jewish friends, including Nathanael West, Dorothy Parker, and Eddie Mayer. One of his *Notebooks* contains the following entry: "Hell, the best friend I have in Hollywood is a Jew—another of my best dozen friends is a Jew. Two of the half dozen men I admire most in America are Jews and two of my half dozen best men in History are Jews. But why do they have to be so damned conceited. That minority conceit—like fairies." 'Nough said.

James edition of the Old and New Testaments, with a note that read "from a friend and colleague of your daughter." Kroll also lets us know that as Christmas 1940 rolled around, Fitzgerald began fretting about a gift for his daughter, Scottie. When Graham generously offered up a new, barely worn fur coat that needed a little altering, Kroll suggested that her father, a furrier, might do the job. And, indeed, Samuel Kroll "remodelled the coat free of charge."

It would be nice to report that Fitzgerald eventually rid himself of anti-Semitic feelings, but it wouldn't be true. As Kroll noted, nothing was simple with Scott. He was a man of insistent contradictions; and with a few drinks under his belt, his darker and more foolish side took over. When drunk, he could sing out "Lily Shiel" and "She's a Jew." Or he might take Kroll aside and confide to her that Graham was "part Jewish," as though he and Kroll were in cahoots.

But he wasn't often drunk, not toward the end, and it's entirely possible that the company of Jewish women made Fitzgerald feel warmer toward Jews in general. And though it was probably nothing more than a tic, he apparently liked going to delicatessens, according to Graham, and ordering knishes because he liked saying "knish." The last word, however, should belong to Kroll, who, I suspect, would not have put up with any anti-Semitic nonsense from him; nor would she have remembered him quite so fondly had he exhibited a virulent bias toward her people: "My memory harbors a gentle man with a nearly collapsed dream whose prevailing gift gave him the strength to keep doing what he did best—to write."

Originally published in the *New Yorker,* July 20, 2015.

Is Cultural Appropriation Ever Appropriate?

Some years ago, I wrote a screenplay about a freed American slave who turned up in London in 1809 and quickly proved himself a boxer capable of wresting the title from the British champion. No small matter, this. England was the only nation on earth where men boxed, and Brits, from hod carriers to earls, naturally considered the sport the province of Englishmen. A Black man contending for the title, especially an *American* Black, was a hard pill to swallow. As one journalist at the time wrote: "It appeared somewhat as a national concern. ALL felt for the honour of their country."

Although I knew a screenplay was a long shot, I thought this particular story had a decent hook—namely, the rise of a free Black community in London and its response to the presence of a loud, brash, powerful African American. His name was Tom Molineaux, and he was no less celebrated and controversial a figure than Jack Johnson or Muhammad Ali. The screenplay kicked around Hollywood for a number of years, but no important agent or producer wanted to take it on. Period pieces, I was informed, were a hard sell, and aside from *Rocky* and *Million Dollar Baby* (with Clint Eastwood starring and directing), boxing pictures didn't do much business.

Then one day the Scottish director Gillies MacKinnon read it. MacKinnon gave me notes and encouraged me to rework it as a TV series. By now cable television had become a magnet for edgy material, and TV executives were finally taking a chance on "Black" projects. Well, my story had plenty of roles for Black actors, and if I integrated (pun mildly intended) more white actors into the story, I could piece together an Upstairs/Downstairs narrative, in which a struggling but thriving Black community in London's East End is set against the scandal-ridden aristocracy of the West End.

So about nine months ago, I turned the screenplay into a treatment for a six-part TV series, broadening its scope to include fictional and historical figures of the Regency period. Currently represented by the largest talent agency in Europe, the treatment is making its rounds of studios, eliciting both enthusiasm as well as regretful demurrals because of prior commitments. Nothing unusual about this, but this time something new had been added to the mix. As one well-known producer put it, the fact that neither the director nor the writer is Black is "a huge red flag." People in the industry, he said, are going to be wary of green-lighting the project.

Yes, it's true, I am engaged in "cultural appropriation," which, according to some moral custodians, makes it both unseemly and illegitimate for a Caucasian, however well meaning, to depict a person of color. I, quite literally, don't have the bloodlines to portray Tom Molineaux, at least not in a creative or fictional format. As it happens, I wrote *about* Molineaux for the *New Yorker* in 1998 on publication of *Black Ajax,* a sly and rambunctious novel by George MacDonald Fraser. Relying on reports by the British press, Fraser presented Molineaux as a brutish simpleton with occasional flashes of insight, whose bad attitude and outrageous behavior are documented by multiple narrators. My screenplay and treatment take a very different tack, and my Molineaux is nothing like Fraser's. Nonetheless, I *am* guilty of putting thoughts into his head and writing dialogue for Black people.

In which case, I am also guilty of theft. According to the legal scholar Susan Scafidi in *Who Owns Culture?,* cultural appropriation refers to "taking intellectual property, traditional knowledge, cultural expressions, or artifacts from someone else's culture without permission. This can include unauthorized use of another culture's dance, dress, music, language, folklore, cuisine, traditional medicine, religious symbols, etc." Needless to say, the "taking" demonstrates a lack of respect and understanding of the exploited materials. I cite this definition because it appears in Lionel Shriver's controversial keynote address at the Brisbane Writers Festival in September 2016. Shriver, who wore a sombrero for part of her talk, argued that she had the right to speak in the voices of people whose culture and ethnicity differed from her own. Otherwise, all she "could write about would be smart-alecky 59-year-old 5-foot-2-inch white women from North Carolina." Upset by the restrictions imposed by cultural arbiters, Shriver confessed that when she started out as a novelist she "didn't hesitate to write black characters . . . or to avail [herself] of black dialects," but now she is "much more anxious about depicting characters of different races, and accents make [her] nervous."

One sympathizes, until she asserts that "membership of a larger group is not an identity. Being Asian is not an identity. Being gay is not an identity. Being deaf, blind, or wheelchair-bound is not an identity, nor is being economically deprived." Really? Because unless one is a Buddhist or the late Derek Parfit, who maintained that identity is too fluid to be any one thing and ultimately doesn't matter, identity is damn well bound up with race, appearance, background, station in life, and ultimately *does* matter—if not to you, then to people who know you. Shriver, however, wasn't being merely provocative; her larger point is that when we embrace narrow, group-based identities too fiercely, "we cling to the very cages in which others would seek to trap us. We pigeonhole ourselves. We limit our own notion of who we are, and in presenting ourselves as one of a membership, a representative of our *type,* an ambassador of an amalgam, we ask not to be seen."

Sounds reasonable. Or does it? It certainly didn't to a twenty-five-year-old Sudanese-Australian woman named Yassmin

Abdel-Magied, who walked out of Shriver's talk, describing it later as "nothing less than a *celebration* of the *unfettered exploitation* of the experiences of others, under the guise of fiction" (her italics). Writing in the *Guardian,* Abdel-Magied accused Shriver of embodying "the kind of attitude that lays the foundation for prejudice, for hate, for genocide"—a not-so-halting statement that makes me think she'd toss my screenplay in a heartbeat, as no doubt would director/producer Lee Daniels, who stated flatly: "I hate white people writing for black people. It's so offensive." Indeed, I suspect that even if I managed to please Daniels, I'd still be an interloper, a talented impressionist doing the police or, in this case, the policed, in different voices.

Although many artists automatically dismiss the arguments of those who seek to censor them, all this angst and anger does have a generative cause: namely, the idea that history gets written by the winners. So "facts" become seen as the shadings and elisions conceived by those with something to gain. All of which suggests that certain topics and themes may "belong" more to one race than another, and that Black writers have a greater moral right to address their heritage than non-Blacks. But does this mean that writers should, as a general rule, avoid writing about people of another race? That ticklish question came to light fifty years ago when William Styron, urged on by his friend James Baldwin, published *The Confessions of Nat Turner.* Styron, a native Virginian with an "absolutely impeccable WASP background," spent six years writing the story of the 1831 bloody revolt of a Virginia slave. Whatever qualms he felt in adopting the voice of a slave were, I imagine, more literary than ethical: Did he have the chops to carry it off? Could he create a believable Black person circa 1830?

Recounting Styron's travails in the September 2016 issue of *Vanity Fair,* Sam Tanenhaus makes the nice point that novelists of

Styron's day believed they could do almost anything, that the very nature of fiction invited them, even challenged them, to explain the United States to itself. Styron attempted to do just that, at least in terms of the antebellum South, and, initially, he thought he'd succeeded. Released in the fall of 1967, *The Confessions of Nat Turner* jumped to the top of the *New York Times* Best Seller list, won the Pulitzer Prize, and earned its author the distinction of being an "expert in the Negro condition." *Life* vied with *Harper's* to run excerpts, and producer David Wolper, who eventually coproduced *Roots,* purchased the movie rights for an unprecedented $600,000.

Styron was riding high, but the praise was short-lived. Six months later, he was regarded by many cultural commentators as a literary carpetbagger who had falsified history while playing into racial stereotypes. Aside from getting some facts wrong, mishandling African American dialect, and not faithfully reproducing the language of early nineteenth-century sermons, Styron had, without any historical evidence, Turner falling in love with Margaret Whitehead, the eighteen-year-old white girl whom he subsequently kills. It's almost as though Styron was courting the disfavor of both Blacks and whites.

In fact, between the time that Styron began writing and the time he finished, the racial landscape had dramatically altered. By the summer of 1967, the civil rights movement had evolved from nonviolent demonstrations in the South to lethal confrontations with the police in urban areas around the country. The ideals of peaceful resistance and mutual coexistence had given way to a Black Power movement more in keeping with Nat Turner's vision of freedom than Dr. King's hopes for a New Jerusalem. And less than a year after the novel's publication, *William Styron's Nat Turner: Ten Black Writers Respond* recorded the many liberties Styron had taken with the facts. He would never again, so far as I know, be commended for his efforts.

Most white writers and academics, I think it's fair to say, liberal or conservative, stood by him. *The Confessions* was a work of fiction, and what errors it contained did not necessarily invalidate it. But if you think there's no gray area here, I suggest that you set aside fifty-five minutes to listen to a discussion between Styron and the Black actor and activist Ossie Davis. The conversation, moderated by James Baldwin, took place on May 28, 1968, and can be heard online. (You know it's a sixties artifact when Baldwin refers to Styron as, "Bill, he's the white cat over here.")

The public discussion was prompted not so much by Styron's novel as by Baldwin and Davis's concerns that a still-to-be-written movie would depict Turner's infatuation with a white teenager —a story line that, according to Davis, could lead to the deaths of young Black men, because "this is one of the areas about which I fear my country can be most immediately psychotic and destructive." The conversation, with occasional input from Baldwin, creates an impression of two well-thought-out positions rather than the give-and-take of a debate. Styron and Davis are unfailingly gracious, self-deprecating, and careful not to disparage the other's views.

Styron wants us to know that an unexpected irony has occurred, since he desired above all else to write "an honest book," in which Nat Turner stands in stark contrast to the individual that Thomas R. Gray, Turner's court-appointed lawyer, depicted in his 1831 five-thousand-word transcript, which purports to be Turner's actual confession. *That* Nat Turner, according to Styron, was a "gifted, intelligent, but totally crazed fanatical butcher" (Turner had, in fact, slaughtered around sixty men, women, and children), whereas *his* simulacrum is "a man of enormous resilience and fantastic vision," "a liberator," and "a hero" who represents what "the human spirit could achieve in overcoming the most ruinous and despotic form of human bondage that men have ever imposed on other men."

Dismayed that people considered his book racist, Styron tries hard to emphasize his laudable intentions. When conceding that his novel ended up doing "some extremely extra-literary things that struck some hideous nerve ends in the public consciousnesses," he sounds like a man who, in skipping a stone across a lake, somehow managed to create a tidal wave. The opprobrium he provoked reminds him of Baldwin's statement that the white man has been on the Black man's back for three hundred years, and he adds wryly that for the past six months he "may be the only white man who has felt that the entire Negro race has been on his back." A choice of words that suggests the enormous gulf between a benign white man and those whose great-grandparents were slaves.

Ossie Davis, to his credit, ignores Styron's clumsiness. Although troubled by Styron's presentation of a sexualized Turner, he's even less keen on Styron's defense of Turner as a heroic Negro. Why should white people presume? Davis's voice at this point seems to take on both an extra treble and more resonance. Styron, he says with suppressed vehemence, "did not feed me something that I culturally need and there is no way he could do it in reality." In fact, one of the things he objects to about *Nat Turner* is "that a white man gave it to [him] in the first place." The Black community, he says, is already speaking a new language, a language forged by experience, whose vocabulary does not conform to white people's expectations, which is one reason the idea of the heroic Black man belongs to Black people first and foremost. As the discussion winds down, the audience doesn't have to figure out who's right because, as Baldwin noted earlier, both men are right.

As for the film that Davis worried about, it finally appeared in 2016, but it was written and directed by an African American, Nate Parker, who made sure that Turner was not "a sexually disturbed lunatic whose sole motivation hinged on his uncontrollable lusts for white women." Parker is no fan of the novel, and though he mischaracterizes it, in my opinion, as overly exploitative, it's easy to see why contemporary writers have refrained from emulating Styron's fictional gambit.*

Frankly, when I began a screenplay about Tom Molineaux back in 2000, it never occurred to me that it might be considered transgressive. *The Confessions of Nat Turner* was old news, and Molineaux was a fascinating figure about whom almost nothing is known. And what a feverish period in British history he lived in. The Regency (1811–20) was rife with fears of wars abroad and the mob at home, and London itself was host to such charismatic characters as the Prince Regent, the MP William Wilberforce, the journalist Pierce Egan, the fashionista Beau Brummell, the smart Lady Melbourne and her fiery daughter-in-law Caroline Lamb, the courtesan Harriette Wilson, as well as Lord Byron and other members of London's sporting set.

Presumably, no eyebrows will be raised when actors playing Byron or Egan speak my words, though one is a low-born Irishman and the other is, well, Byron. But Black people, apparently, are off limits, which is too bad, since there were some fourteen or fifteen thousand Africans living in London, with their own stores, eateries, churches, and civic organizations. Surely they must have been

---

*Gone are the days when Bernard Malamud (*The Tenants*), Richard Price (*Clockers*), and Philip Roth (*The Human Stain*) could write Black characters and not have their knuckles rapped. Should a white writer today have the effrontery to assume the identity of a Black man, as Michael Chabon did in his 2012 novel *Telegraph Hill,* it would not go unpunished. In a generally admiring review in the *New York Times,* Michiko Kakutani felt the need to reprimand Chabon for sometimes "trying very hard 'to sound like he was from the 'hood.'" Other critics also felt it incumbent either to chide Chabon for his hubris or to confess that they, as white readers, could not say whether he had gotten the racial angle right.

stunned, worried, and gratified by that swaggering young Black man from the United States who had the audacity to challenge the champion and everything the champion stood for. (God, it must have felt good to knock England on its ass.)

All this is dramatic tinder—and who better than I to light it, steeped as I am in the period? Naturally it is much more complicated than that. How could I, a Jewish boy born in Sweden and raised in New York, understand the experience of a Black slave? Well, I could do what fiction writers usually do and enter imaginatively into his head, just as I would with a white character. If I did a poor job, I'd suffer the same fate as Styron, and I was OK with that. I also accepted the fact that I'd be given less leeway than a Black writer. What was more difficult to accept is that I wouldn't even be allowed to fail.

Yet why should Black writers better imagine Molineaux's cast of mind? Black people were not merely an oppressed minority in 1810, they were legally considered chattel, supposedly incapable of finer emotions, and thus undeserving of normal human rights. Do you really have to be Black to get it? Many ethnic groups, including my own, have at one time or another been enslaved or been the victims of genocide. The truth is, it isn't bondage that is unimaginable, or suffering, or the evil men do to one another, it's the absurd ethos that justifies slavery. But while I maintain that it's no more credible for a Black writer to re-create Molineaux's London than a white one, I also feel compelled to add that I am probably the wrong person to represent the experience of Black people closer to my own day.

I don't say any of this lightly. The history of racial relations in the United States is, of course, appalling. Between 1880 and 1940, around four thousand Black Americans were lynched, sometimes in front of hundreds or thousands of spectators. Segregation was about more than exclusion; it reflected deeply held beliefs and fears about genetics, sexuality, intelligence, and social hierarchies. Those who joined the civil rights movement were not just demanding the right to vote, or to obtain an education, or to sit at lunch counters, or to drink from water fountains, or even to exist existentially as free men and women. When Black people marched in 1963 and 1964 in Alabama and Mississippi—and were pummeled and injured and killed—it was because they sought to realign a moral universe, a universe unwilling to budge. It takes guts to face down people who hate you, but it requires a profound commitment, perhaps even grace, to oppose not just the Man but a history in which love of country is equated with the separation of the races. And out of respect for that experience, alien to me in a way that prejudice and suffering are not, I would hesitate to write from the point of view of a Black man or woman involved in the civil rights movement.

That said, time has a way of, if not modulating events, allowing the common humanity of very different experiences to emerge. The fact that Tom Molineaux lived at a time when conventional thinking dictated that Black people were genetically inferior to whites is reason enough for people of all races to write about him. One isn't so much trying to get into the skin of someone else as endeavoring to show the absurdity of racial assumptions. And though young writers are enjoined to "write what you know," it's not especially useful advice when one doesn't know much. Because it's not experience, but what one does with it that makes someone worth reading. Clearly, I don't know what it's like to be Black *or* white in 1810 and fight for the championship of England, but then, who does?

The more salient point is that Nat Turner was allowed to tell his story before he died, whereas Tom Molineaux's story consists only in what British journalists said about him; and in both cases, a certain skepticism is advisable. Molineaux's story, however, begs for amplification, and I, for one, believe I can speak for him as well as I could for a Jew who lived in Spain around AD 1600 or in Italy in 1935. No doubt there are any number of people who know more about the Regency than I do, and a smaller number who know more about the free Black community in London around 1810, and a smaller number still who are familiar with the London Prize Ring, but I'm pretty sure that none of them knows as much as I do about all three subjects. Does this make me qualified to write about Molineaux? In a word, yes. Whether I do a good job, of course, remains to be seen.

It may not be politic to say it, but politics—whether of the left or the right—should not prevent writers from loosening their imagination. Unpleasant or not, their choice of subject or approach to it is part of our democratic fabric, and when we discourage writers from writing, we are, in effect, strangling artistic freedom. What's more, we're repudiating plain old human sympathy. Empathy exists. It exists because pain, humiliation, suffering, and powerlessness are universal. The particulars may differ, but the sympathetic imagination discerns the common humanity in all inhuman acts.

Styron must have believed this as well. He thought he was writing on the side of the angels, for only a deep-rooted innocence can account for his inserting a white love interest where none had in fact existed. No one should begrudge him his labor, though we have every right to judge the result. In the end, it's the result that matters, not the person who achieves it. So, if a Black writer or a Chinese writer or an Egyptian writer wants to write about the Holocaust, which decimated my family, then may the Muse be with you. What do I care about your ethnicity or background as long as you do justice to what happened? It isn't cultural affiliation alone that does justice to injustice, that creates art from

A Pleasure to Read You

If we are to believe Deborah Mitford, Duchess of Devonshire, her father, Lord Redesdale, read only one book in his life and that was *White Fang*. "He loved it so much that he never read another. 'Dangerous good book,' he used to say; 'no point in trying any more.'" I also loved *White Fang,* but instead of desisting from books, I couldn't wait to get my hands on more of them. Of course, I was barely a teenager at the time, and since then I've come across a few novels even better than *White Fang*—and some worse.

Nonetheless, Lord Redesdale, father of the notorious Mitford sisters, two of whom wrote novels that he presumably opened, had a point. Reading ought to be pleasurable, so why waste time on poems or novels that don't provide any? A plausible enough conceit that only becomes bothersome when we attempt to define reading pleasure. Should we even begin or is the subject a spiraling Escheresque staircase whose ending is everywhere and nowhere? Pleasure? Surely no sane critic would approach the subject, not anymore, not today.

Frank Kermode was eminently reasonable and almost dishearteningly well read, but he took it on, in 2004, in two lectures delivered at the University of California, Berkeley. The lectures were later published as *Pleasure and Change: The Aesthetics of Canon,* boosted by commentaries from professors Geoffrey Hartman and John Guillory and theater director Carey Perloff. All too aware that the canon, as the product of privilege, is suspect by the very qualities that have traditionally defined literature, Kermode uses the word "canonical" advisedly, tapping books partly because of the pleasure that is "a necessary though not obvious requirement of the canonical."

Aware, too, that pleasure is a sticky subject, Kermode glances at Barthes's *Le plaisir du texte,* which divides the delighted reader's response into pleasure and *jouissance,* the latter issuing from a sense of blissful interruption caused by something sensual and unexpected. He also quotes the Czech critic Jan Mukarovsky, who believed "that part of pleasure . . . is likely to lie in the power of the object to transgress, to depart, interestingly and revealingly, from the accepted way of such artifacts."

Kermode himself thinks the term "dismay" nicely encapsulates a reader's pleasurable response to a text. It's a dismay predicated on our ability to recognize the interruption, comprehend the revealing departure, and appreciate its implications. What all these interested parties are saying is that a successful work of literature depends on a successful reading of its contents, and that the pleasure involved derives from the text's power to immerse us, enchant us, surprise us, and teach us. So far so good. But how do I know that you find the same pleasure in the same lines, passages, and books that I do?

It can't be helped—unanswerable questions have to be asked: Does one kind of literature afford a more refined pleasure than another kind? Can we compare the pleasure induced by Virginia Woolf to, say, that induced by Agatha Christie? Is "Casey at the Bat" potentially less (or more) enjoyable than Keats's "Ode to Autumn"? Is the pleasure of reading Henry James similar to that of reading George Eliot? At what point does a story's eloquence or lack of it begin to affect people in the same way? Surely, Lord Redesdale would feel little of the dismay favored by Kermode when perusing Wordsworth's "Resolution and Independence," a poem that Kermode believes holds pleasures for the informed reader.

Pleasure is, indeed, a loaded term, both too restrictive and too vague to convey all the possible responses to art. At times, one may feel Hume's disinterestedness in the well made; other times, one might be overcome by Burke's awe of the sublime. Instead of pleasure, there are pleasures: delightful, thrilling, reflective, exhilarating, sensual, appreciative, cathartic, and so on. Nonetheless, one can't help but feel that expertise also yields a certain pleasure. Those who skate well, ski well, shoot well, and, yes, read well experience a kind of pleasure unavailable to the less proficient.

Remains only to prove that reading is a skill. I mean, of course, the reading of prose and poetry where skill is conterminous with the recognition of what is not only well executed (devoid of clichés, shopworn observations, useless modifiers, etc.) but also capable of the dismay that depends on knowledge of previous works, the better to discern both originality and difference. This is, one hesitates to say, a more complicated or "higher" form of pleasure, which fifty years ago critics like Kermode took for granted.

In fact, his treatise, whose staid title, *Pleasure and Change,* belies the dynamism it espouses, is an argument for cogent reading. Drawing our attention to Wordsworth's use of rhyme royal and his improvisations on Spenser and Chatterton, Kermode wants us to understand what makes "Resolution and Independence" transgressive. Of significance here, however, is not only our ability to spot something old but the work's ability to achieve something new while seducing us through metrical proficiency and power of observation. After all, if the gift isn't worth unwrapping, it really doesn't matter what departures or references we recognize.

Now, every reader will have his or her list of favorite poems and novels, including those that impressed us when we were adolescents and may still raise goose bumps thirty or sixty years later. Sometimes the pleasure fades; sometimes it intensifies: life has a way of changing how we feel about both people and books. So there may come a day when "Stately plump Buck Mulligan" won't make me smile; when P. G. Wodehouse's stories will leave me cold; when Dylan Thomas's "craft and sullen art" won't produce an admiring gasp. Until then, however, I'll judge new poems and novels by the sound and sense of books that have become imprinted on my memory.

How one responds to literature depends on what one has responded to before encountering the *idea* of literature. That is, we read before we've been taught what is supposedly good to read. And, naturally, we do not all have the same inclination to read, or equal leisure to read, or, to be blunt, the same aptitude for reading. Not everyone is meant to enjoy books that require more discernment than *White Fang.*

Me, I'd like to enjoy *White Fang* again, but I think it's a nonstarter. I place the blame partly on temperament and partly on my education. When I was one-and-twenty and studying literature in 1968, I wasn't given much choice about what to read. It was Shakespeare and—not or—Milton. It was Donne *and* Dryden. It was as many of the Elizabethans and Augustans and Romantics and Victorians and modernists that could fit on the syllabus. Writers we didn't study in class we were encouraged to read in private. Moreover, fiction and poetry were supplemented by a healthy dose of criticism: Erich Auerbach's *Mimesis;* Northrop Frye's *Anatomy of Criticism;* T. S. Eliot's essay "Tradition and the Individual Talent"; Lionel Trilling's anthology *The Experience of Literature;* Ian Watt's *The Rise of the Novel;* William Empson's *Seven Types of Ambiguity;* René Wellek and Austin Warren's *Theory of Literature;* as well as books by Ernst Robert Curtius, I. A. Richards, Mario Praz, F. R. Leavis, J. Hillis Miller, M. H. Abrams, Georg Lukács, et al.

I'm not claiming that everything in these texts is indisputable or that literature cannot be understood without them. I'm simply suggesting that these critics—and even those engaged in the New

Criticism—saw poems and novels as historically situated, revealing the leanings and swervings and divagations among various writers. What they taught me, what they inoculated in my brain stem, was an appreciation of a literary tradition that evolved as the world evolved, whose fluctuations in style and theme always spoke in some way to earlier works.

In this pre-postmodern world, we focused on a writer's performance; how he produced his effects; what she learned from her precursors; how he or she made us see the world and literature differently. The starting point was the work itself rather than any theoretical claims made for it. Such a curriculum was not necessarily more rigorous or demanding than what transpired in English departments afterward, but it did produce a bracing aesthetic insularity. Works of literature belonged to something called "literature," and if writers didn't pay their dues—responding to and deviating from precursors—membership was denied them.

In a canon, Kermode writes, "each member of it fully exists only in the company of others; one member qualifies or nurtures another." In other words, literature is essentially an ongoing conversation, an idea wittily reinforced by Borges's edict that "every writer creates his own precursors. His work modifies our conception of the past, as it will modify the future. . . . The early Kafka of 'Betrachtung' [his first collection of stories] is less a precursor of the Kafka of somber myths and atrocious institutions than is Browning or Lord Dunsany." In effect, Browning is more Kafkaesque than the early Kafka. How's that for dismay?

Were we more innocent then? Sure. We did not read in terms of colonialism, sex, race, cultural anthropology, psychological heuristics, or the philosophical prescripts that questioned the very act of interpretation. Each of which, I hasten to add, has augmented our understanding of literature. But it's not an understanding that embraces the idea of dismay except in the condemnatory sense of books disappointing us because they hold views we no longer find conscionable or forgivable. Although it's natural to think that broadening the canon (or dismissing it entirely) increases the store of available pleasure, one has to consider the quality of that pleasure.

Something, I fear, goes missing when the historical particularity of style is dropped from the curriculum. That aesthetic exchange whereby writers strive to outdo their precursors (vividly traced by Harold Bloom and W. Jackson Bate) has taken a back seat to more socially pressing concerns. Although serious writers continue to write good books, interesting books, unusual books, literature itself is now viewed primarily as a cultural artifact defined by sex, race, and class. It acts more as a critique of society than as a gloss on previous work. To take a well-worn example: Conrad's *Heart of Darkness* is invariably seen as a racial and colonialist work of fiction. No one is saying that the story is not well told. Nonetheless, it is bad in a way that is more important than the ways it is good.

Recently, the novelist Jesmyn Ward, writing in the *New York Times Book Review* (April 12, 2018), gracefully extolled the virtues of *The Great Gatsby* while focusing on Gatsby's exclusionary status as though it were the novel's most important feature: "the idea most invisible to [her] as a young reader [was] that the very social class that embodied the dream Gatsby wanted for himself was predicated on exclusion. . . . He'd been born on the outside; he would die on the outside." But what reader past the age of fourteen doesn't get this? It's not that Ward is wrong; it's just that harping on Jay Gatz's displacement conveniently lines up with our culture's need to condemn privilege.

I may be overreaching, but this emphasis on the socioeconomic aspect of the novel suggests that we're in danger of losing a category of pleasure. If what is *most* important in a book is its attitude toward imperialism or class or injustice, then we automatically consign good writing to secondary status. *Gatsby* is great not because James Gatz is an interloper who exposes class prejudice, but because Fitzgerald learned from Conrad (as well as from Booth Tarkington, Sherwood Anderson, and Compton Mackenzie). Wanting to be a great writer, he had to be his own writer, and with *Gatsby,* he aspired to "write something *new*—something extraordinary and beautiful and simple + intricately patterned." And part of the pleasure of reading *Gatsby* is discovering where and how he differed from the writers he admired.

That said, arguments against a purely aesthetic approach to art are legitimate. Not only because canon formation reflected the views of educated white males, but also because when you come down to it, who's to say what makes a poem or novel truly great? After all, criticism is never absolute and therefore always imprecise. John Gross, author of the excellent *The Rise and Fall of the Man of Letters,* tells us that when Lamb, Hazlitt, and Carlyle were writing for magazines and literary reviews, their pages were "unashamed vehicles for party propaganda, often of the narrowest kind, and generally too overbearing and coarse-grained in their approach to encourage criticism of much depth."

So how do we reconcile the idea of the Great Books with the cronyism, personal antipathy, stupidity, spite, and greed that all played a part in sustaining that idea? Simply put, you take note and then move on. Because whatever built-in bias prevailed in canon formation, whatever self-interest motivated writers and critics, what *really* mattered was the act of departure that distinguished one poet from another. Without writers wanting desperately to distinguish themselves, our literature would be, at best, an enjoyably inert affair, summoning neither joy nor dismay.

To be clear, I'm not suggesting that a cursory or superficial literary education precludes enjoyment of books. In fact, it may help, as Lord Redesdale intuited. I'm simply wondering if the knowledge that corrals pleasure from the Great Books (and let's just admit that some poetry and prose is great) doesn't also diminish the amount of pleasure we can mine from ordinary and unoriginal work. "Bad writing," to quote Tom Waits, "is destroying the quality of our suffering"—in which case, doesn't it also reduce the quality of our enjoyment?

These aren't statements I can back up with proof. Tastes differ and taste dictates. Moreover, cultural and social mores change, and older generations continue to find fault with the generations coming up. Loss is the main complaint: loss of innocence, loss of intimacy, loss of interest in what matters, loss of skill in pursuing what matters. Writers in particular like to envision a saner, more stimulating age in which to have lived, but it's hard to know if life or art afforded more pleasure in the past.

May I venture something true but not profound? There is nothing doctrinaire about pleasure; it will come when it will. But one thing is certain: You must first love what gives you the deepest pleasure. Therefore, we might tentatively liken reading pleasure to sexual intimacy, where intimacy is heightened by love based in part on familiarity with another person. Analogously, a love of literature (with its own sort of familiarity) adds to the intensity of the reading experience. Precious as it may sound, the more literary the reader (the more he or she knows about literature), the deeper his or her pleasure will be. No one wants to say it, but some pleasures aren't procurable by everyone. Although I listen to Bach and am moved by the *St. John Passion,* I'm quite sure I don't hear his music as well as a classically trained musician. In fact, I believe that such a person "hears" Bach better, enjoys him more, and appreciates him on a deeper level.

To return to Kermode, I wonder how many younger readers could take pleasure in his little book, whose polished arguments revolve around dozens of poets and writers whose works are referenced by its contributors. This breadth of learning does not so much prove an aesthetic canon as it suggests common reference points that bookish people continue to discuss. Simply because there is no aesthetic compass showing true north does not mean that an artistic north does not exist. It just fluctuates when we try to pinpoint its exact location. But that's no reason to give up the search, for it's only when we stop believing that it lies over the next ridge that the literary map formed by Homer, Dante, Chaucer, and Shakespeare begins to fade and come apart.

Originally published in the *American Scholar,* Winter 2019.

John Ashbery, the Poet of Our Clime

Now that the elegiac dust is beginning to settle, perhaps we can step back and ask what he meant to us. For a poet who made even sophisticated readers knit their brows, who never, despite his awards and honors, captured the public's imagination, he was for students of poetry someone whose existence was part of our existence and whose death in September 2017 came as a double blow. We felt not only the loss of a singular poetic voice but also the passing of a cultural era. For along with Richard Wilbur, he was the last of the major poets to emerge in the middle of the twentieth century and was—with the possible exception of Seamus Heaney—the foremost English-speaking poet of his day.

Like Whitman, Frost, Eliot, Stevens, Dickinson, and William Carlos Williams, John Ashbery had a hand in creating the American poem. And when he died at the age of ninety, the encomiums actually exceeded expectations. Even his admirers liked him. Indeed, no poet in recent memory—not Merrill or Walcott, not Strand, Wilbur, or Kinnell—generated the coupling of such affection and respect. It was something to behold, this gentle blizzard of appreciation.

In person he was, by all accounts, shy, modest, funny, erudite, and literary to his core. In his work, he could be winsome, goofy, evocative, boring, and amusing, with a fluency of language that seemed both familiar and newly minted. He was chameleonlike but always recognizably himself. He could be serious and stark, but also whimsical. In fact, he made whimsy into a potent force, which kind of defeats the idea of whimsy, but never mind. His detractors, of whom there were a few, thought many of the poems were more frosting than cake. And some poems were that. But many more were not.

I confess I was one of the naysayers. But now that his living voice has been stilled, the voices in his poems speak a beat more gaily. More tenderly as well. It may be that the passing of the years, as well as his passing, have led me to reconsider the work. Like Ezra Pound, who, after years of resistance, came to the sane conclusion that Whitman had much to offer, I also acknowledge that "I am old enough now to make friends."

> It was you that broke the new wood,
> Now is a time for carving.
> We have one sap and one root—
> Let there be commerce between us.

Such commerce, however, does not begin with acceptance, but with questioning. Like many readers, I often wondered not only what I was reading but also why I was reading him. Yes, he had a way with words, but often the words left me indifferent or confused. Ashbery, of course, was famous for his impenetrability—a fact that both surprised and annoyed him. Reflecting on the critical response to his poem "Litany," he remarked, "I'm quite puzzled by my work too, along with a lot of other people. I was always intrigued by it, but at the same time a little apprehensive and sort of embarrassed about annoying the same critics who are always annoyed by my work. I'm kind of sorry that I cause so much grief."

From any other poet these words might seem disingenuous. But if Ashbery felt bad, he also wrote as he pleased. Indeed it was a guiding principle of his writing. In a statement prepared for the encyclopedia *Contemporary Poets* (1975), he explained, "There are no themes or subjects in the usual sense, except the very broad one of an individual consciousness confronting or confronted by a world of external phenomena. The work is a very complex but, I hope, clear and concrete transcript of the impressions left by these phenomena on that consciousness. The outlook is Romantic. Characteristic devices are ellipses, frequent changes of tone, voice (that is, the narrator's voice), point of view, to give an impression of flux."

Flux. Not usually something one turns to poetry for, but that's exactly what Ashbery aspired to, because, as he told Bryan Appleyard in the London *Times:* "I don't find any direct statements in life. My poetry imitates or reproduces the way knowledge or awareness comes to me, which is by fits and starts and by indirection. I don't think poetry arranged in neat patterns would reflect that situation. My poetry is disjunct, but then so is life." Fair enough, but is it fair to the reader? Reasonable as it may sound, such a justification for art rings hollow. Knowledge begins with experience, as Kant wrote, but "it does not follow that it arises out of experience." In fact, without the ordering structures of the mind, sensations would remain unintelligible, which is why we necessarily perceive "objects," and objects have order, order has value, and so knowledge is valid.

I bring up Kant not to add a dollop of pretentiousness to my reading of Ashbery, but because Ashbery himself, while a student at Harvard in the 1940s, jotted in his notebook, "Kant stinks," presciently settling on his own view of experience. The man had a philosophical streak, managing to work "epistemological" into one famous poem and to adduce William James in still another, wrapping up with: "Still, there's a lot of fun to be had in the gaps between ideas. / That's what they're made for! Now I want you to go out there / and enjoy yourself, and yes, enjoy your philosophy of life, too. / They don't come along every day. Look out! There's a big one."

Read enough Ashbery and you know this is more a humorous caution than a humorous embrace of big ideas. So how does one represent flux when mind and language yearn for order and stability? Obliquely is the answer, and Ashbery in time mastered the art of approaching life (in poetry) slantwise:

> The windows are open again
> The dust blows through
> A diagram of a room.
> This is where it all
> Had to take place,
> Around a drum of living,
> The motion by which a life
> May be known and recognized,
> A shipwreck seen from the shore,
> A puzzling column of figures.
> . . .
>
> You are
> So perversely evasive

His work *can* be evasive and often frustrating, but it represents a different esoterica than that of other "difficult" poets. With Donne, Eliot, and Stevens, one feels that the effort to figure out what they're saying is essential to realizing some important philosophical/theological truth. With Ashbery, not so much. Instead, we think, "Oh, so that's what he meant. OK, then." Learning what he means adds to our enjoyment, but it's not as though something much greater is at stake. Ashbery isn't shooting for profundity or certainty; in fact, he's temperamentally inclined to head in the other direction: to show the flux of things as filtered through the changeable medium of the observer himself.

What strikes me is that readers of poetry were perfectly fine with this. They didn't care that they didn't know what he was talking about, which, you have to admit, is a pretty sweet deal for a writer. And because Ashbery's work gives the impression of being simultaneously offhanded and impenetrable, it lends itself to so many pronouncements that even contradictory views sound true. By refusing to impose an arbitrary order on the world, Ashbery invites his critics to apply their own sense of order. So Paul Auster in *Harper's* focuses on Ashbery's "ability to undermine our certainties, to articulate so fully the ambiguous zones of our consciousness." Other critics maintain that "difficulty" itself is Ashbery's answer to the dilemma of living (perhaps in the way that the barbarians in Cavafy's famous poem were a solution). Or it could be that Ashbery's poems are simply about poetry itself, about the wavering intersection of art and life, about finding the poem as you write the poem.

In any event, after the publication of *Self-Portrait in a Convex Mirror* (1975), which won the Pulitzer Prize, the National Book Award, and the National Book Critics Circle Award, he could have written almost anything and have it acclaimed by serious readers, much as Picasso dashed off sketches on napkins to pay for dinner. I'm not suggesting that Ashbery didn't put in the time and effort, just that he probably didn't have to, since coherence was not the point.

The question remains: Why did we grant him license to puzzle us? Why was he permitted to engage in what another poet called an "intolerable vagueness"? The fact that he was a dab hand with cadence and composition does not by itself explain why we readily accepted his elisions, asides, cute figures of speech, pop culture references, and the arbitrary inclusion of things around him (a telephone ringing, a bird alighting on the windowsill). Given these rhetorical tics, how did he become the logical incarnation of the postmodernist poet who legitimately crossed that porous line into solipsism (much as Joyce had done a half century earlier) and, furthermore, brought us along without complaint?

Although sui generis, he did not emerge from nowhere. His skein of influences—the French surrealists, the abstract expressionists, collage, atonal music, his confreres of the New York school of poets, and such literary precursors as Whitman, Stevens, and Marianne Moore—suggests a grand synthesis of many styles and ideas, yet his work, for the most part, seems a cross between derring-do and nonchalance, a balance of wit and melancholy. There is a genuine modesty about the poems, the best of which attain a lighthearted majesty:

> But there is in that gaze a combination
> Of tenderness, amusement and regret, so powerful
> In its restraint that one cannot look for long.
> The secret is too plain. The pity of it smarts,
> Makes hot tears spurt: that the soul is not a soul,
> Has no secret, is small, and it fits
> Its hollow perfectly: its room, our moment of attention.
> That is the tune but there are no words.
> The words are only speculation
> (From the Latin *speculum,* mirror):
> They seek and cannot find the meaning of the music.
> We see only postures of the dream,
> Riders of the motion that swings the face
> Into view under evening skies, with no
> False disarray as proof of authenticity.

But this, too, doesn't explain his reputation or why we happily took him up (excepting, of course, for those who never came around to his enigmatic artistry). Although I am now convinced there are enough decorative phrasings sluicing through the work to merit the claims made for it, I also believe it was the context of the times that set him on his prosodic course and encouraged us to follow him. This is not something self-evident or even demonstrable but is part of what Lionel Trilling called the hum and buzz of culture, a feeling in the air composed of academic trends, philosophic attitudes, public discourse, and the recognition of scientific and technological innovations.

Goethe coined a more specific late eighteenth-century version of this: "Epoche der forcierten Talente entsprang aus der Philosophischen." All that remains is to determine just what the current philosophical temper is and how Ashbery embodies it. I intend no glibness by this. Indeed, I think that toward the last quarter of the last century a way of thinking emerged that might account for our embrace of Ashbery's cruciverbalist poetry. If forced to sum it up, I think it has a predominately neurological component or, more accurately, it reflects the ascendance of the biological and neurological sciences in the ways we think about thinking.

Because the human brain has evolved to the point that we can scan it, we've learned that it is responsible for—well, just about everything we think, say, and do. How we perceive, the preferences we exhibit, and the cognitive miracles and limitations that define us are all by-products of the brain's activity. Although it has long been known that human beings look for patterns in nature, research by the likes of Daniel Kahneman and Abraham Twerski has also shown that we often imagine and misunderstand such patterns. Evidently, our cognitive biases dissuade us from understanding such biases. For example, our tendency to categorize prevents us from seeing the fuzziness of boundaries. And a tendency to predict future probabilities based on past events often influences our decisions without our carefully weighing the true odds.

Such intuitive biases come into play because we process experience in ways that may not reflect reality. Furthermore, there are scores of such biases, which obviously increase the probability of errors. I, myself, may be writing this in the grip of "confirmation bias"—that is, favoring or interpreting information so that it confirms my own preconceptions. Ashbery didn't have to know their appellations to know that cognitive biases are part of our neural circuitry. Somehow he sensed that the brain contra Kant can fool itself by structuring what it perceives; and because it misleads us and because experience is never static, a philosopher like Derek Parfit can surmise that identity itself is a convenient fiction, since we are continually, if not consciously, evolving.

Although we're predisposed to create plausible narratives of cause and effect, we also tolerate and even embrace complexity and chance. And why shouldn't we? We live in an information-soaked, rapidly traversed, and rapidly changing natural and technological universe, where anything can happen and often does—from unpredictable acts of terrorism to the election of a presumably unelectable presidential candidate. There is no reality that cannot be unexpectedly altered. Indeed, it seems almost vulgar to regard anything with an absolute belief in its unassailabilty. Permanence and stability seem as outmoded as Newtonian mechanics.

Perhaps weirder still is the fact that this doesn't discombobulate us—that, in fact, it has a practical application. I take my cue from Nassim Nicholas Taleb, distinguished professor of risk engineering at New York University's School of Engineering and author of *The Black Swan* and *Fooled by Randomness.* Taleb is all in favor of randomness, believing that regarding it as a risk "is the central illusion in life." Randomness is salutary not because it offers a rebuke to the sameness of things, but because systems sometimes "get stuck in a dangerous impasse" and "randomness and only randomness can unlock them and set them free." Casting a cold eye on what passes for the scientific method, Taleb, who numbers among his influences Kahneman and Karl Popper, has no trouble fitting chance and luck into his worldview; he even thinks that "systems are sometimes stabilized from an injection of confusion."

Fluidity, ambiguity, the tenuousness of identity all show up in Ashbery's work, not to mention randomness. Out of nowhere, a burst of the trite or mundane: "No soap," "lawyering up," "Heck, it was anybody's story," "it was nobody's biz." Who can deny the randomness in the ordinary course of events? And Ashbery, allusiveness notwithstanding, is the poet of the ordinary. He always was. Pondering Andrew Marvell's "The Mower to the Glow-Worms" for a college English course, he wrote: "The things we do in our daily life, the thoughts we have, they have meaning, they are us, for as long as they last, and when they fade and other things take their place, they still have their meaning in us, even if we're not aware of them." A quarter of a century later his feelings haven't changed: "For although memories, of a season, for example, / Melt into a single snapshot, one cannot guard, treasure / That stalled moment. It too is flowing, fleeting."

Nothing that I've said actually explains the appeal of Ashbery's poetry, but it does offer a reason why we make fewer logical demands on it. The world is stranger and more fragmented (Internet or no Internet) than ever before, and like every serious poet before him, Ashbery offers a gloss on his age—with one important difference: whereas poets in the past advocated for, or consciously reflected, an implicit worldview regarding "the starry skies above and the moral law within," the majority of Ashbery's poems are resolutely unsystematic, unbeholden to an intellectual cause or creed, often carrying their own dichotomies with them.

Something
Ought to be written about how this affects
You when you write poetry:
The extreme austerity of an almost empty mind

Colliding with the lush, Rousseau-like foliage of its desire to
communicate,
Something between breaths, if only for the sake
Of others and their desire to understand you and desert you
For other centers of communication, so that understanding
May begin, and in doing so be undone

Ashbery doesn't set himself up as a communication center, but he does want to convey how poetry ("a hopelessly minor art") can express the inexpressible ties between living, thinking, writing. It wasn't enough to extend the tradition of the ontological subtleties of Stevens, the plainspokenness of William Carlos Williams, or the binary inflections of W. H. Auden. Ashbery wanted poetry to be about both the process of creation and the person who creates. "There should be no program," Robert Creeley reports him saying. "The poem, as we imagined it, should be the possibility of everything we have as experience. There should be no limit of a programmatic order."

Any summation of Ashbery's oeuvre, however, is notoriously difficult; the man simply tested too many bodies of water when learning how to swim. He'd majored in English literature at Harvard and did his honors thesis on Auden. As a doctoral candidate at Columbia, he focused on Henry Green; and in his application for a Guggenheim, he stipulated that "[Raymond] Roussel's literary interests closely parallel my own." Later, inspiration came from Luciano Berio's *Omaggio a Joyce,* children's books, pulp novels, *Life* magazine, and atonal music. Could he do in verse what John Cage did in music? What the abstract expressionists did on canvas? After listening to Anton Webern, he wondered if he could "isolate a particular word, as you would isolate a particular note, to feel it in a new way."

It's good to be open. It's also good to be closed to certain intellectual trends. One of the outcomes of modernism was a heightened appreciation of the limits of art. How was one to proceed after the Dadaists, cubists, surrealists, projectivists, imagists, constructivists, and vorticists had their say? Although neither Pound nor Joyce put a crimp in literary work (hard to muffle those who feel the need to speak), Braque, Picasso, Mondrian, Kandinsky, Stravinsky, Bruckner, and Schoenberg put into question the validity of harmonic music and representational painting. So artists looking to strike out in a new direction began to think about the medium itself. I'm simplifying, but for second-generation modernists (including the young Ashbery), art with a capital A became problematic. One could no longer compose or paint without acknowledging a medium's essence.

Explaining the thinking behind abstract expressionism, the critic Harold Rosenberg imagined artists claiming, "My painting is not Art; it's an Is. It's not a picture of a thing; it's the thing itself. It doesn't reproduce Nature; it is Nature." Rosenberg was skeptical of such work, and with good reason. If I may be permitted a Yogi Berra-ism: just because there's no place to go doesn't mean you have to go there. But artists, of course, did go, and the results were uneven. If some of Ashbery's early poetry was about the art of poetry, he was in a sense emulating the work of atonal composers and abstract expressionists.

In the Charles Eliot Norton Lectures he delivered at Harvard (subsequently published in 2000 as *Other Traditions*), Ashbery chose six "minor" writers who, he acknowledged, helped jump-start his own work. They are, in order of appearance, John Clare, Thomas Lovell Beddoes, Raymond Roussel, John Wheelwright, Laura Riding, and David Schubert. Anyone who has ever transcribed for publication a formal address will envy the book's flow of ideas and judicious asides. Ashbery is an excellent guide to these writers' work and provides wonderful capsule biographies. But what comes through is not how gifted these writers are (though he makes a nice case for them), but how they bolstered the sense of his own vocation. "I don't know what it says about my own poetry that I like these poets; whether it means that I wish to be given 'special treatment,' or that for some reason I like writing that isn't simple, where there is more than at first glance meets the eye—or both."

Just in case we still weren't sure, *Other Traditions* reminds us that Ashbery was not interested in writing the perfect poem. Instead, he sympathizes with John Clare, "whose habit, one might even say whose strength, was imperfect." Ashbery welcomed imperfection, not because he found it charming, but because it's an element of thought. One doesn't always think logically or sequentially, so one needn't pretend to. Which works if you're John Ashbery, but not very well for you or me.

After quoting approvingly Schubert's lines "But the poem is just this / Speaking of what cannot be said / To the person I want to say it," Ashbery acknowledges, almost casually, that he "enjoy[s] Schubert more than Pound or Eliot." And part of what he enjoys is that Schubert's work "manages to render itself immune to critical analysis or even paraphrase." This is, needless to say, a tactical shift in taste about modernist poetry, whose value we associated with the textual analysis of Jarrell, Blackmur, Wilson, Tate, and Winters. Ashbery doesn't dismiss formalist poets; he just prefers the poem that can't be pinned down. As did Laura Riding, I imagine that he, too, would caution readers "not to construe my poems as poetry in the generally understood sense of the term."

It's this temperamental attraction to the offbeat and eccentric that drew Ashbery to the literary antics and self-referential strategies of Roussel, Duchamp, and Apollinaire. We're not talking Jabberwocky silly or Ogden Nash–like noodlings. The French writers were both playful and deadly earnest about their non-sense; it shored up a philosophical approach to life, which, I'm afraid to say, wears thin the older one grows, although Tristan Tzara's amiable poem "To Make a Poem" reads like early Ashbery. Nonetheless, after a certain age, one may be excused for ho-humming conceptual art and the linguistic playfulness of the avant-garde. Indeed, one may find an earlier French writer, who also dabbled in the ridiculous, more congenial: "Tirez le rideau, la farce est jouée." But before it's over, it has meaning; it matters. And if a work of art is to matter, it has to matter to people other than the artist. In short, a work that takes its audience only to the end of the artist's own mind is simply an intellectual exercise. How many people attend a performance of John Cage's *4′33″* more than once?

All this is to say—what probably will annoy his admirers—that Ashbery succeeds despite his influences. For good and for ill, he liked to experiment, and experiment, by implication, contains the possibility of failure. Reviewing *The Tennis Court Oath* (1962), John Simon observed that Ashbery "has perfected his verse to the point where it never deviates into—nothing so square as sense!—sensibility, sensuality, or sentences." Even critics sympathetic to Ashbery's modus operandi shook their heads at his willful evasions. As late as 1990, Dana Gioia, acknowledging Ashbery's unique sound, his "gift of felicitous, natural phrasing," concluded that "he is a marvelous minor poet, but an uncomfortable major one."

No such doubts troubled Helen Vendler and Harold Bloom, who championed Ashbery's verse early in his career. Bloom, as is his wont, expressed such enthusiasm that it made readers like me suspicious: "How it ravished my heart away the moment I heard it!" Bloom said of "Wet Casements." "Certainly when I recite that poem myself and remember the original experience of hearing [Ashbery] deliver it, it's hard to see how any poem could be more adequate." Really? One has to wonder what the hell Bloom is hearing when reciting such lines as: "A digest of their correct impressions of / Their self-analytical attitudes overlaid by your / Ghostly transparent face," which seem to me prolix, crowded, and—why not say it—bad?

But it's OK that Ashbery doesn't always hit the mark. Why should he? We measure a poet by his best work, not his worst or middling efforts. All great poets have their "Queen Mab," and what does Shelley's failed attempt mean when measured against "Ozymandias," supposedly executed between dessert and a digestif? Poets are rather like baseball players in this regard. If they bat over .300 lifetime, they're candidates for the Hall of Fame. And the more often poets step up to the plate, the more likely they'll ground out or get a routine hit. And Ashbery, it seems to me, got in more licks than any contemporary poet—more than thirty volumes—and his batting average is better than respectable.

Because Ashbery was curious, adventurous, and interested in seeing what he could pull off, Vendler could assert, "Rarely has an exquisite writer deliberately written so badly." Which is to say that he occasionally liked to botch a good job. But it isn't the occasional badness of the poems that bothers me; it's the demands the good ones make. All his evocative lines cannot tamp down my resentment of their inaccessibility. If a writer doesn't mind ignoring the comfort level of the common reader, then he shouldn't mind provoking the reader's disapproval. "The demand that I make of my reader," James Joyce informed Max Eastman, "is that he should devote his whole life to reading my works." I beg to differ. I have no desire to join a cult, even a cult devoted to Joyce. I'll go as far as *Ulysses* because, after all, the man wrote *A Portrait* and *Dubliners,* but someone else will have to wade through *Finnegans Wake,* which no doubt is also a work of genius. Nonetheless, I'll be damned if I'm going to let Joyce convince me. Why should another mind so subjugate my mind to his? Genius always deserves a break, but not necessarily our time.

If I seem to be equivocating, I suppose I am—not because I want to minimize Ashbery's achievement, but because I want to enjoy it without being guided by highfalutin explanations as to why I should enjoy it. More literary criticism has been spent on Ashbery's work than on any other contemporary poet's, and much of it is a valiant effort to justify its lack of clarity. His admirers recommend that it's best to read him in the spirit of something's happening, though we don't know what it is, do we Mr. Ashbery? Mustering Whitman, Stevens, and other poets, critics run through Ashbery's influences as though that alone were sufficient to validate his work. They intelligently examine the poems and convince themselves that clarity is not the same as meaning, and that meaning is less important than sound. As Richard Kostelanetz put it in 1976, "The real key to Ashbery's genius lies, in my opinion, in the 'sound' of his poetry. . . . His poetry initially communicates, as music communicates, at levels that defy conceptual definition. . . . The mastering of it becomes a kind of spiritual experience."

Well, that might depend on whom you ask. No such outcome has thus far repaid my efforts. Nor do I wish it to. There's no denying Ashbery's pleasing rhythms and fluency even when his subject matter might have merited a more austere approach, but I'm not sure that his music is what defines him. Poets have been claiming that music supersedes meaning (or is poetry's meaning) ever since Baudelaire first heard Wagner in 1860. Verlaine, Eliot, Valéry, Pound, and Graves have all touched on the musical element in verse as something apart from pure *technē,* but perhaps Frost put it most succinctly: "Look after the sound and the sense will take care of itself." Good advice if you have something to say. But sound, while indispensable, is not always sufficient, which is why bookish people took exception to Bob Dylan (wonderful as his early songs are) winning the Nobel Prize for literature. And Ashbery, like all notable poets, is about more than sound. Indeed, listening to him read, one might be surprised by the level tone, the lack of affect. His rendering of "Self-Portrait in a Convex Mirror" perhaps not ironically puts me in mind of a knowledgeable docent, someone whose engine is stuck in neutral.

I like what Meghan O'Rourke had to say about him: "He is the first poet to achieve something utterly new by completely doubting the possibility—and the value—of capturing what the lyric poem has traditionally tried to capture: a crystallization of a moment in time, an epiphanic realization—what Wordsworth called 'spots of time.'" She's right, I think. And when she says that at his best he "succeeds better than any other writer at conveying how the barrage [of language] affects a mind haunted by its own processes and by the unstable patterns that shape-shift around us," she describes him perfectly. But then I think that the satisfactory explanation of a poem does not make it a satisfactory poem.

Ashbery made mistakes, but they were mistakes he had to make. He was, as Karin Roffman's recent biography informs us, a mix of naked ambition and self-effacement, determined to succeed on his own terms while remaining dubious of his own efforts. He was his own best enemy. His education and wide reading, his intimate knowledge of poetry, his curiosity, his early years in Paris, his attunement to midcentury developments in all the arts, both stymied and drove him to write. But write what? Write how? Open to all things, he became the first poet conspicuously to view himself as both the subject and the object of his work. (Were they not the same thing?) The world could be known only through himself, so why bother aspiring to objectivity or universality?

Eliot began to teach us that lesson almost one hundred years ago: the idea that poetry is not, as he himself once stated, an escape from personality, but rather is the personal, which allows the poet to venture inward unburdened by the conventional rules of prosody. Consider the dismay even literary people felt on encountering these lines in 1922:

> Summer surprised us, coming over the Starnbergersee,
> With a shower of rain; we stopped in the colonnade,
> And went on in sunlight, into the Hofgarten,

> And drank coffee, and talked for an hour.
> *Bin gar keine Russin, stamm' aus Litauen, echt deutsch.*
> And when we were children, staying at the archduke's,
> My cousin's, he took me out on a sled,
> And I was frightened. He said, Marie,
> Marie, hold on tight. And down we went.
> In the mountains, there you feel free.
> I read, much of the night, and go south in the winter.

The changes in subject and pronouns, and the expectation that readers would follow the narrator's jumble of thoughts, must have struck a chord with Ashbery. Ashbery has his own music, but surely Eliot showed him how to hold the instrument. With so much to absorb in the fifties, with all the talk about the meaning of life and art and individual responsibility (it was, after all, the time of phenomenologists and existentialists), a poet intent on saying something new in a new way was almost directed to turn inward. But in Ashbery's case it wasn't, as with many memoirists and minor poets, a headlong rush into significance. Rather it was a sidelong, almost apologetic foray into the mind's workings. ("Still, it is the personal, / interior life that gives us something to think about. / The rest is only drama.") His role was to be aware of himself reacting to things and ideas and to record the mind's perambulations. That's the voice he had to find, and he did. His best poems seem to say, "Here is a poem, but it's also just me talking to you":

> So much has passed through my mind this morning
> That I can give you but a dim account of it:
> It is already after lunch, the men are returning to their positions
>   around the cement mixer
> And I try to sort out what has happened to me. The bundle of
>   Gerard's letters,

And that awful bit of news buried on the back page of yesterday's
paper.
Then the news of you this morning, in the snow. Sometimes the
interval
Of bad news is so brisk that . . .

or

Evening waves slap rudely at the pilings
and birds are more numerous than usual.
There are some who find me sloppy, others
for whom I seem too well-groomed. I'd like to strike
a happy medium, but style
is such a personal thing, an everlasting riddle.

or

Somewhere someone is traveling furiously toward you,
At incredible speed, traveling day and night,
Through blizzards and desert heat, across torrents, through narrow
passes.
But will he know where to find you,
Recognize you when he sees you,
Give you the thing he has for you?

More than any other contemporary writer, he angles words in ways we haven't quite seen before. Nor does form inhibit him (see "Le livre est sur la table" or "Hotel Lautréamont"); he can do his precursors and something else besides, and one reason we accept his rhetorical quirks is that we know he can write otherwise but chooses not to. We also know that in his seamless integration of thoughts and images he is a poet unlike any other, a poet who, for all his peccadilloes, somehow ends up more comforting than perplexing. And maybe on some level we don't wish to understand. Not to understand what ostensibly has meaning suggests that there is something greater to be understood. After all, there's precious little comfort in a random universe that is a mere accident of matter exploding out of Nothingness, a gigantic slip on the nonexistent banana into some-thingness where bananas come to be. So perhaps randomness is, as Taleb claims, a necessary corrective precisely because it has no clear or decipherable meaning.

What does this have to do with poetry? Only that we don't have to understand everything about a poem in order to enjoy it, provided that we trust the poet's intelligence and intuition. It's better not to be party to a plan than to think that there is no plan. That's why we can enjoy a sequence of disparate images in David Lynch's *Twin Peaks* and why we happily sing Dylan's lyrics without quite knowing what they mean. Although no sustained work of art comes to pass without due deliberation and craftsmanship, there are occasions when the symbiosis of consciousness and unconsciousness produces a mysterious beauty immune to deconstruction. Not every poet gets there, but Ashbery did. His best poems affirm Eliot's adage "Genuine poetry can communicate before it is understood."

Originally published in *Raritan,* Summer 2019.

Old News

WHY WE CAN'T TELL THE TRUTH ABOUT AGING

In days of old, when most people didn't live to be old, there were very few notable works about old age, and those were penned by writers who were themselves not very old. Chaucer was around fifty when "The Merchant's Tale" was conceived; Shakespeare either forty-one or forty-two when he wrote *King Lear,* Swift fifty-five or so when gleefully depicting the immortal but ailing Struldbruggs, and Tennyson a mere twenty-four when he began "Tithonus" and completed "Ulysses," his great anthem to an aging but "hungry heart."

One might think that forty was not so young in Shakespeare's day, but if you survived birth, infections, wars, and pestilence, you stood a decent chance of reaching an advanced age no matter when you were born. Average life expectancy was indeed a sorry number for the greater part of history (for Americans born as late as 1900, it wasn't even fifty), which may be one reason that people didn't write books about aging: there weren't enough old folks around to sample them. But now that more people on the planet are over sixty-five than under five, an army of readers stands waiting to learn what old age has in store.

Reading through a recent spate of books that deal with aging, one might forget that, half a century ago, the elderly were, as V. S. Pritchett noted in his 1964 introduction to Muriel Spark's novel *Memento Mori,* "the great suppressed and censored subject of contemporary society, the one we do not care to face." Not only are we facing it today; we're also putting the best face on it that we possibly can. Our senior years are evidently a time to celebrate ourselves and the wonderful things to come: traveling, volunteering, canoodling, acquiring new skills, and so on. No one, it seems, wants to disparage old age. Nora Ephron's *I Feel Bad about My Neck* tries, but is too wittily mournful to have real angst. Instead, we get such cheerful tidings as Mary Pipher's *Women Rowing North: Navigating Life's Currents and Flourishing as We Age,* Marc E. Agronin's *The End of Old Age: Living a Longer, More Purposeful Life,* Alan D. Castel's *Better with Age: The Psychology of Successful Aging,* Ashton Applewhite's *This Chair Rocks: A Manifesto against Ageism,* and Carl Honoré's *Bolder: Making the Most of Our Longer Lives*—five chatty accounts meant to reassure us that getting old just means that we have to work harder at staying young.

Pipher is a clinical psychologist who is attentive to women over sixty, whose minds and bodies, she asserts, are steadily being devalued. She is sometimes tiresomely trite, urging women to "conceptualize all experiences in positive ways," but invariably sympathetic. Agronin, described perhaps confusingly as "a geriatric psychiatrist" (he's in his mid-fifties), believes that aging not only "brings strength" but is also "the most profound thing we accomplish in life." Castel, a professor of psychology at UCLA, believes in "successful aging" and seeks to show us how it can be achieved. And Applewhite, who calls herself an "author and activist," doesn't just inveigh against stereotypes; she wants to nuke them, replacing terms like "seniors" and "the elderly" with "olders." Olders, she believes, can get down with the best of them. Retirement homes "are hotbeds of lust and romance," she writes. "Sex and arousal do change, but often for the better." Could be, though I've never heard anyone testify to this. Perhaps the epicurean philosopher Rodney Dangerfield (who died a month short of his eighty-third birthday), having studied the relationship between sexuality and longevity, said it best: "I'm at the age where food has taken the place of sex in my life. In fact, I've just had a mirror put over my kitchen table."

Applewhite makes an appearance in Honoré's book. She tells Honoré, a Canadian journalist who is now fifty-one, that aging is "like falling in love or motherhood." Honoré reminds us that "history is full of folks smashing it in later life." Smashers include Sophocles, Michelangelo, Rembrandt, Bach, and Edison, who filed patents into his eighties. Perhaps because Honoré isn't an American, he omits Satchel Paige, who pitched in the majors until he was fifty-nine. Like Applewhite, who claims that the older brain works "in a more synchronized way," Honoré contends that aging may "alter the structure of the brain in ways that boost creativity."

These authors aren't blind to the perils of aging; they just prefer to see the upside. All maintain that seniors are more comfortable in their own skins, experiencing, Applewhite says, "less social anxiety, and fewer social phobias." There's some evidence for this. The connection between happiness and aging—following the success of books like Jonathan Rauch's *The Happiness Curve: Why Life Gets Better after 50* and John Leland's *Happiness Is a Choice You Make: Lessons from a Year among the Oldest Old,* both published last year—has very nearly come to be accepted as fact. According to a 2011 Gallup survey, happiness follows the U-shaped curve first proposed in a 2008 study by the economists David Blanchflower and Andrew Oswald. They found that people's sense of well-being was highest in childhood and old age, with a perceptible dip around midlife.

Lately, however, the curve has invited skepticism. Apparently, its trajectory holds true mainly in countries where the median wage is high and people tend to live longer or, alternatively, where the poor feel resentment more keenly during middle age and don't mind saying so. But there may be a simpler explanation: Perhaps the people who participate in such surveys are those whose lives tend to follow the curve, while people who feel miserable at seventy or eighty, whose ennui is offset only by brooding over unrealized expectations, don't even bother to open such questionnaires.

One strategy of these books is to emphasize that aging is natural and therefore good, an idea that harks back to Plato, who lived to be around eighty and thought philosophy best suited to men of more mature years (women, no matter their age, could not think metaphysically). His most famous student, Aristotle, had a different opinion; his *Ars rhetorica* contains long passages denouncing old men as miserly, cowardly, cynical, loquacious, and temperamentally chilly. (Aristotle thought that the body lost heat as it aged.) These gruff views were formed during the first part of Aristotle's life, and we don't know if they changed before he died at the age of sixty-two. The nature-is-always-right argument found its most eloquent spokesperson in the Roman statesman Cicero, who was sixty-two when he wrote *De senectute,* liberally translated as "How to Grow Old," a valiant performance that both John Adams (dead at ninety) and Benjamin Franklin (dead at eighty-four) thought highly of. Cicero mentions knowing men who lived to a ripe old age, but then gives the game away by admitting he never "heard of an old man who forgot where he hid his money."

Montaigne took a more measured view. Writing around 1580, he considered the end of a long life to be "rare, extraordinary, and singular . . . 'tis the last and extremest sort of dying: and the more remote, the less to be hoped for." Montaigne, who never reached sixty, might have changed his mind upon learning that, in the twenty-first century, people routinely live into their seventies and eighties. But I suspect that he'd still say, "Whoever saw old age, that did not applaud the past, and condemn the present times?" No happiness curve for him.

There is, of course, a chance that you may be happier at eighty than you were at twenty or forty, but you're going to feel much worse. I know this because two recent books provide a sobering look at what happens to the human body as the years pile up. Elizabeth Blackburn and Elissa Epel's *The Telomere Effect: A Revolutionary Approach to Living Younger, Healthier, Longer* and Sue Armstrong's *Borrowed Time: The Science of How and Why We Age* describe what is essentially a messy business. Armstrong, a British science and health writer, presents the high points of aging research along with capsule biographies of the main players, while Blackburn, one of three recipients of the 2009 Nobel Prize in Physiology, focuses on the shortening of telomeres, those tiny aglets of DNA attached to our chromosomes, whose length is a measure of cellular health. Telomeres, Blackburn writes, "hate processed meats like hot dogs." What do they like? Anything that affects the production of telomerase, the enzyme that replenishes those little aglets of DNA, such as nutritious eating, exercise, and meditation. As for smoking, better not.

Basically, most cells divide and replicate some fifty-plus times before becoming senescent. Not nearly as inactive as the name suggests, senescent cells contribute to chronic inflammation and interfere with protective collagens. Meanwhile, telomeres shorten with each cell division, even as lifestyle affects the degree of shrinkage. Data now suggest that "married people, or people living with a partner, have longer telomeres."

Walt Whitman, who never married, made it to seventy-two, and offered a lyric case for aging. "*YOUTH,* large, lusty, loving—youth full of grace, force, fascination," he intoned. "Do you know that Old Age may come after you with equal grace, force, fascination?" It's pretty to think so, but the biology suggests otherwise. The so-called epigenetic clock, as it continues to strike the hour, shows our DNA getting gummed up: age-related mitochondrial mutations reduce the cells' ability to generate energy, and our immune system slowly grows less efficient. Bones weaken, eyes strain, hearts flag. Bladders empty too often, bowels not often enough, and toxic proteins build up in the brain to form the plaque and the spaghettilike tangles associated with Alzheimer's disease. Not surprisingly, 68 percent of Medicare beneficiaries today have multiple chronic conditions. Not a lot of grace, force, or fascination in that.

The marginalization of the elderly was never a secret. Nor did we bother in the past to apologize for it. Although the elderly were not necessarily shamed in earlier centuries—Homer thought one Nestor was worth ten men like Ajax—we didn't exactly provide for them. The general approach to aging was one of professed respect but of little attention. It's hard to put a date on when policy began to change. Social Security in 1935 was a step in the right direction, yet the psychiatrist Robert Neil Butler felt the need to coin the term "ageism" in 1968 to deplore the conditions that old people without means had to contend with in America, a situation still in need of reform, as Atul Gawande reminded us some years ago in *Being Mortal.* Gawande's concern is with end-of-life care, but if treatment follows attitude, he's also fighting to change Applewhite's perception that no one "blinks when older people are described as worthless."

In short, the optimistic narrative of pro-aging writers doesn't line up with the dark story told by the human body. But maybe that's not the point. "There is only one solution if old age is not to be an absurd parody of our former life," Simone de Beauvoir wrote in her expansive 1970 study *The Coming of Age,* "and that is to go on pursuing ends that give our existence a meaning—devotion to individuals, to groups, or to causes—social, political, intellectual, or creative work." But such meaning is not easily gained. In 1975 Butler published *Why Survive? Being Old in America,* a Pulitzer Prize–winning study of society's dereliction toward the nation's aging population. "For many elderly Americans old age is a tragedy, a period of quiet despair, deprivation, desolation and muted rage," he concluded.

Four years later, the British journalist Ronald Blythe, who must be one of the few living writers to have spoken to the last

Victorians (he's now just shy of ninety-seven), had a more sanguine perspective.* His *The View in Winter,* containing oral histories of men and women at the end of their lives, is a lovely, sometimes personal, sometimes scholarly testament that reaches "no single conclusion. . . . Old age is full of death and full of life. It is a tolerable achievement and it is a disaster. It transcends desire and it taunts it. It is long enough and it is far from being long enough." Some years after that, the great Chicago radio host Studs Terkel, who died at ninety-six, issued an American version of Blythe's wintry landscape. In *Coming of Age* (1995), Terkel interrogated seventy-four "graybeards" (men and women over the age of seventy) for their thoughts on aging, politics, and the American way of life.

Now that we're living longer, we have the time to write books about living longer—so many, in fact, that the Canadian critic Constance Rooke, in 1992, coined the term "Vollendungsroman," a somewhat awkward complement to "Bildungsroman," to describe novels about the end of life, such as Barbara Pym's *Quartet in Autumn,* Kingsley Amis's *The Old Devils,* and Wallace Stegner's *The Spectator Bird.* Since then, plenty of elderly protagonists have shown up in novels by Louis Begley (*About Schmidt*), Sue Miller (*The Distinguished Guest*), Saul Bellow (*Ravelstein*), Philip Roth (*Everyman*), and Margaret Drabble (*The Dark Flood Rises*). The realm of nonfiction has more than kept pace.† And, as was bound to happen, gerontology meets the Internet in *Aging and the*

* Sadly, Mr. Blythe died in January 2023.

† Today, there's a website that lists the top fifty books on aging, which, alas, omits William Ian Miller's eccentric *Losing It: In Which an Aging Professor Laments His Shrinking Brain* (2011); Lynne Segal's judicious but tough-minded *Out of Time: The Pleasures and the Perils of Ageing* (2013); and Martha C. Nussbaum and Saul Levmore's smart, provocative *Aging Thoughtfully: Conversations about Retirement, Romance, Wrinkles, and Regret* (2017), in which a philosopher and a law professor discuss everything from *Lear* to the transmission of assets.

Digital Life Course, a collection of essays edited by David Prendergast and Chiara Garattini (2017). The library on old age has grown so voluminous that the fifty million Americans over the age of sixty-five could spend the rest of their lives reading such books, even as lusty retirees and power-lifting septuagenarians turn out new ones.

The most recent grand philosophical overview of aging is also by a woman, and lighting upon Helen Small's *The Long Life* (2007) is like entering the University of Old Age after matriculating at a perfectly good college. Small, an Oxford don (and just forty-two when the book came out), wants to integrate old age into how we think about life. Pondering what it means to be someone who has completed a life cycle that Montaigne thought unnatural, she considers old age to be "connected into larger philosophical considerations," whose depiction, whether literary or scientific, both drives and reflects emotional and ethical attitudes. And, echoing the philosopher Bernard Williams, she suggests that our lives accrue meaning over time, and therefore the story of the self is not complete until it experiences old age—the stage of life that helps us grasp who we are and what our life has meant.

Not everyone wants to find out if Small's equation between old age and self-knowledge holds up. In 2014 the *Atlantic* ran an essay by the oncologist and bioethicist Ezekiel J. Emanuel, then fifty-seven, whose title alone, "Why I Hope to Die at 75," caused an uneasy shuffling among seventy-year-olds. Emanuel believes that, by the time he hits this milestone, he will have lived a full life. He argues that by seventy-five "creativity, originality, and productivity are pretty much gone for the vast, vast majority of us." Unlike Honoré and Applewhite, Emanuel thinks that "it is difficult, if not impossible, to generate new, creative thoughts, because we don't develop a new set of neural connections that can supersede the existing network." Although he doesn't plan on suicide, he won't actively prolong his life: no more cancer-screening tests (colonoscopies and the like); no pacemaker or stents. He wants to get out while the getting is good.

It's an unselfish outlook, but not quite credible to unevolved people like me. Having entered my seventies, I don't care that I may not have much to contribute after I'm seventy-five. I'm not sure I'll have had that much to contribute *before* turning seventy-five. Also, Emanuel seems to be talking about artists, intellectuals, and scientists who will be pained by the prospect that their brain power and creativity may ebb in their twilight years, and not about your average working stiff who, after decades of toiling in factories or offices, may want to spend more time golfing or reading books about golf. A grudging admiration for the good doctor ultimately gives way to disappointment when he reserves the right to change his mind, thereby confirming Montaigne's gloomy projection that "our desires incessantly grow young again; we are always re-beginning to live."

Let's grant that there are as many ways to grow old as there are people going about it, especially since more of us keep chugging along despite our aches and ailments. "If I'd known I was going to live this long," said Mickey Mantle (or possibly Mae West or Eubie Blake), "I would have taken better care of myself." Mantle was only sixty-three when he died, but the truth is that many of us are going to be physically much better off at eighty than Shakespeare's Jaques could have imagined—*avec* teeth, *avec* sight, and *avec* hearing (which is to say: dental implants, glasses, and hearing aids). A long life is a gift. But I'm not sure we're going to be grateful for it.

Normal aging is bad enough, but things become dire if dementia develops, the chances of which double every five years past the age of sixty-five. Applewhite, however, citing recent research, no longer thinks that dementia is "inevitable, or even likely." May she live long and prosper, but for those of us who have cared for spouses or parents with dementia, it's not always a simple matter to know on whom the burden falls the heaviest. (One in three caregivers is sixty-five or older.)

Obviously, I'm not a candidate for the Old Person's Hall of Fame. In fact, I plan to be a tattered coat upon a stick, nervously awaiting the second oblivion, which I'm reasonably certain will not have the same outcome as the first. Nonetheless, I like to think that I have some objectivity about what it's like to grow old. My father lived to be almost 103, and most of my friends are now in their seventies. It may be risky to impugn the worthiness of old age, but I'll take my cane to anyone who tries to stop me. At the moment, we seem to be compensating for past transgressions: far from devaluing old age, we assign it value it may not possess. Yes, we should live as long as possible, barring illness and infirmity, but when it comes to the depredations of age, let's not lose candor along with muscle tone. The goal, you could say, is to live long enough to think: I've lived long enough.

One would, of course, like to approach old age with grace and fortitude, but old age makes it difficult. Those who feel that it's a welcome respite from the passions, anxieties, and troubles of youth or middle age are either very lucky or inordinately reasonable. Why rail against the inevitable—what good will it do? None at all. Complaining is both pointless and unseemly. Existence itself may be pointless and unseemly. No wonder we wonder at the meaning of it all. "At first we want life to be romantic; later, to be bearable; finally, to be understandable," Louise Bogan wrote. Professor Small would agree, and though I am a fan of her book, I have my doubts about whether the piling on of years really does add to our understanding of life. Doesn't Regan say of her raging royal father, "'Tis the infirmity of his age: yet he hath ever but slenderly known himself"? The years may broaden experience and tint perspective, but is wisdom or contentment certain to follow?

A contented old age probably depends on what we were like before we became old. Vain, self-centered people will likely find aging less tolerable than those who seek meaning in life by helping others. And those fortunate enough to have lived a full and productive life may exit without undue regret. But if you're someone who—oh, for the sake of argument—is unpleasantly surprised that people in their forties or fifties give you a seat on the bus, or that your doctors are forty years younger than you are, you just might resent time's insistent drumbeat. Sure, there's life in the old boy yet, but certain restrictions apply. The body—tired, aching, shrinking—now often embarrasses us. Many older men have to pee right after they pee, and many older women pee whenever they sneeze. Pipher and company might simply say "Gesundheit" and urge us on. Life, they insist, doesn't necessarily get worse after seventy or eighty. But it does, you know. I don't care how many seniors are loosening their bedsprings every night; something is missing.

It's not just energy or sexual prowess but the thrill of anticipation. Even if you're single, can you ever feel again the rush of excitement that comes with the first brush of the lips, the first moment when clothes drop to the floor? Who the hell wants to tear his or her clothes off at seventy-five? Now we dim the lights and fold our slacks and hope we don't look too soft, too wrinkled, too old. Yes, mature love allows for physical imperfections, but wouldn't we rather be desired for our beauty than forgiven for our flaws? These may seem like shallow regrets, and yet the loss of pleasure in one's own body, the loss of pleasure in knowing that one's body pleases others, is a real one.

I can already hear the objections: If my children are grown and happy; if my grandchildren light up when they see me; if I'm healthy and financially secure; if I'm reasonably satisfied with what I've accomplished; if I feel more comfortable now that I no longer have to prove myself—why, then, the loss of youth is a fair trade-off. Those are a lot of ifs, but never mind. We should all make peace with aging. And so my hat is off to Dr. Oliver Sacks, who chose to regard old age as "a time of leisure and freedom, freed from the factitious urgencies of earlier days, free to explore whatever I wish, and to bind the thoughts and feelings of a lifetime together." At eighty-two, he rediscovered the joy of gefilte fish, which, as he noted, would usher him out of life as it had ushered him into it.

"No wise man ever wished to be younger," Swift asserted, never having met me. But this doesn't mean that we have to see old age as something other than what it is. It may complete us, but in doing so it defeats us. "Life is slow dying," Philip Larkin wrote before he stopped dying, at sixty-three—a truth that young people, who are too busy living, cavalierly ignore. Should it give them pause, they'll discover that just about every book on the subject advocates a "positive" attitude toward aging in order to maintain a sense of satisfaction and to achieve a measure of wisdom. And yet it seems to me that a person can be both wise and unhappy, wise and regretful, and even wise and dubious about the wisdom of growing old.

When Socrates declared that philosophy is the practice of dying, he was saying that thought itself is shaped by mortality, and it's because our existence is limited that we're able to think past those limits. Time has us in its grip, and so we devise stories of an afterlife in which we exist unshackled by days and years and the decay they represent. But where does that get us, beyond the vague suspicion that immortality—at least in the shape of the vengeful Yahweh or the spiteful Greek and Roman gods—is no guarantee of wisdom? Then again, if you're the sort of person who sees the glass as one-eighth full rather than seven-eighths empty, you might not worry about such matters. Instead, you'll greet each new day with gratitude, despite coughing up phlegm and tossing down a dozen pills.

But what do I know? I'm just one person, who at seventy-one doesn't feel as good as he did at sixty-one, and who is fairly certain that he's going to feel even worse at eighty-one. I simply know what men and women have always known: "One generation passeth away, and another generation cometh: but the earth abideth forever." If only the writer had stopped there. Unfortunately, he went on to add, "In much wisdom is much grief: and he that increaseth knowledge increaseth sorrow. . . . The fate of the fool will overtake me also. What then do I gain by being wise? This too is meaningless." No young person could have written that.

Originally published in the *New Yorker,* October 28, 2019.

A Coda

Learning about the process of aging is not for the faint of heart, even though heart cells, like nerve and red blood cells, are nondividing. Aging is all about cells, and the genes, chromosomes, and proteins scheming within. All of which is catnip to molecular biologists who don't see why the process cannot be slowed or even reversed. The science of turning back the biological clock began in the third quarter of the twentieth century and is already extremely complicated. Not content to view old age simply as an amalgam of age-related diseases, researchers began to search for one or two underlying causes across a spectrum of interrelated pathologies.

An excellent guide to this history is Sue Armstrong's *Borrowed Time,* which lets us know that a few impediments stand in the way—for example, genetic damage, mitochondrial dysfunction, stem-cell exhaustion, telomere attrition, oxidative stress, and the breakdown of cellular communication. We're only as healthy as our cells, and our cells are programmed to get old and sick. A senescent cell formed when we're eighteen gets bounced; formed at seventy, it tends to stick around and produce cytokines that contribute to chronic inflammation.

Armstrong isn't trying to scare us, but she also doesn't spare us the ways that our innate and adaptive immune systems progressively become less efficient at getting rid of senescent cells. For instance, neutrophils, our most populous white blood cells, which move through blood vessel walls to reach tissues suffering injury or infection, eventually lose their sense of direction. "Blundering neutrophils," Armstrong calls them. Meanwhile, the dendritic cells of the adaptive immune system, which collect and deliver bits and pieces of foreign microbes to bone and thymus cells (which use the information to repel the invaders), also grow old and tired. When Philip Roth characterized old age not as a battle but as a massacre, he was thinking about the death of friends, but it was *their* dying cells that caused him to mourn.

Given what we know about how the body breaks down, shouldn't we be able to delay or prevent it? We're trying, certainly: rejuvenating senescent cells or killing them off with senolytic drugs or tinkering with the mechanism that keeps them going. Recombinant DNA technology can now create pluripotent stem cells that have the potential to replace senescent cells and to fix the mechanism that causes them to self-destruct.

Indeed, we've learned to regulate cellular degeneration in mice through maintenance and repair, much as structural engineers repair the girders of a bridge as they gradually erode. Indeed, we've reversed age-associated decline in elderly mice, though at a cost to the subjects who were stitched together (parabiosis) in order to study the effects of mingling old and young circulation systems. Armstrong, incidentally, goes out of her way to assure us that parabiosis is achieved with as little pain and stress as is humanely possible. Still, the aging of mice and men is different. To stop cellular senescence, inflammation, and the depletion of B and T cells in humans, we have to alter or make sure that the information contained in the DNA of pertinent genes reaches the cells it's designed for.

All this research into reversing the aging process looks extremely promising. Reputable scientists who resemble neither Boris Karloff nor Bela Lugosi can modify specific genes to create stem cells that have the potential to become virtually any kind of specialized cell, especially those lost to senescence. The idea that there are people alive today who may live to be 150 and older is no longer science fiction. Wolf Reik, a molecular biologist and professor of epigenetics at the University of Cambridge, states unequivocally that "the potential for reversing aging is absolutely there," and Gordon Lithgow of the Buck Institute for Research on Aging in Novato, California, maintains that we've reached an "Alexander Fleming moment," albeit noting that an interval of ten years occurred between the discovery and the manufacturing of penicillin.

It's tricky to predict these things. Aging isn't only messy, it's also full of subtle and not-so-subtle trade-offs. For all the harm that senescent cells do, they also release molecules that help repair and regenerate other cells and protect against the growth of tumors. As for the cells that help us when we're young, some develop harmful traits when we're old, thus making aging an "enjoy now, pay later" sort of transaction. So whenever we decide to modify the human genome in order to prolong our enjoyment, we may be going against nature itself.

It may not be nice to fool Mother Nature, as the old margarine commercial had it, but it's also not particularly easy. There are risks involved in introducing new cells, and epigenetic modifications can have unintended consequences since people's biological clocks are set differently. Not only do we respond differently to the same stimuli, but epigenetic patterns vary among individuals, among different tissues within an individual, and even among different cells. All of which makes a cellular Shangri-La a hard-to-reach destination spot. Fiddling with the human genome will undoubtedly improve and prolong life, but as Armstrong cautions, there probably won't be one medical solution that works equally well for all people.

An Improbable Friendship

In the autumn of 1934, Jacques Barzun, a twenty-six-year-old assistant professor of history, and Lionel Trilling, an assistant professor of English and comparative literature, sixteen months older, began to teach together at Columbia University. The course, for selected upperclassmen, was called rather grandly "The Colloquium on Important Books." It convened on Wednesday evenings for two hours and soon became the place to be in Morningside Heights. If students wanted seriousness and intellectual sizzle, they sat for an interview and hoped to be found worthy.

Twelve years later, Barzun and Trilling hooked up again, this time to lead a graduate seminar, "Studies in European Intellectual History and Culture since 1750," aka "The Seminar on the Great Books." In addition to canonical poets and novelists, the syllabus included John Stuart Mill's ruminations on Bentham and Coleridge, Chesterton's *The Victorian Age in Literature,* Burke's *Reflections on the Revolution in France,* Bagehot's *The English Constitution,* and Freud's *Civilization and Its Discontents.* Like the colloquium, the seminar soon attained legendary status both inside and outside academia. So popular did it become that Fred Friendly, an executive producer at CBS News, tried (and failed) to persuade them to offer a version of it for television. (Not an invitation one suspects that Leslie Moonves would extend today.)

For four decades, until Trilling's death in 1975, the two men remained friends, a considerable achievement, since intellectuals aren't famous for their amiability. Wordsworth and Coleridge were great friends for a while until the lordly Wordsworth decided that the scattered Coleridge was too much to bear. Emerson and Thoreau were friends for ten years, but then drifted apart for unspecified reasons. Goethe and Schiller had a famous collaborative friendship, but Schiller died after eleven years. And Byron and Shelley's friendship ended with Shelley's drowning in 1822. Closer to our own day, Hemingway and John Dos Passos split over differences incurred during the Spanish Civil War, and Norman Podhoretz (who attended the colloquium) dropped, and was dropped by, several well-known writers, including Norman Mailer and Allen Ginsberg.

Literary friendships probably wear best when a certain distance is maintained. Robert Lowell and Elizabeth Bishop's warm friendship was more epistolary than proximal; and Henry James and Edith Wharton, both reserved in manner, never came to blows, as far as we know. Barzun and Trilling, however, saw a lot of one another. They taught at the same table, saw each other socially, and founded, with W. H. Auden, The Readers' Subscription Book Club—but, according to Barzun, never experienced "in forty-three years of weekly conferrings a single moment of irritation."

And yet nothing about them matched. Barzun was born in France in 1907; Trilling in New York in 1905. Barzun, whose parents were patrons of the arts, grew up in Paris and Grenoble among the European avant-garde. Trilling's father was a tailor from Białystok, Poland, who had immigrated to Queens. Barzun's father was a diplomat who settled for a time in New Rochelle. Barzun was a nonpracticing Catholic; Trilling a secular but self-affirming Jew (becoming in 1939 the first Jewish professor granted tenure by the English and comparative literature department).

As students and instructors at Columbia they had only a nodding acquaintance. Barzun, tall, fair-haired, Gallically handsome, was self-assured and interested in history, theater, music, and detective stories. Trilling, shy, intense, on the short side, was keen on Freud, Marx, and American fiction. To a budding and brooding intellectual like Trilling, the young Barzun seemed too comfortable in his own skin; there was no angst, no alienation. "Such awareness as we first had of each other," Trilling recalled, "was across a barrier which had about it something of a barricade." Meanwhile, in Barzun's eyes, Trilling seemed "content to do well, with little exertion, in what he liked and to stumble through the rest." Upon learning they would be paired up, neither one jumped at the prospect.

But their anxiety about teaching together soon disappeared. Their differences complemented rather than distanced them. Trilling gravitated toward the oblique, self-conscious narratives of modernism, while Barzun liked to roam, surveying the fixtures that both created and weakened society. Aloof, unruffled, grounded in the empirical, Barzun's "masters in criticism" were Gautier, Hazlitt, Poe, Goethe, and Nietzsche, writers, he thought, Trilling was "untouched by." For Barzun, the essence of culture was "interpenetration"; for Trilling, culture was something that defined you, even in your attempts to deny its influence. Students didn't have a chance. If one didn't catch you out in a mistake, the other one would.

Their respective teaching styles were summed up in Jeffrey Hart's recollections of his student days at Columbia: "Barzun clarifying, usually trying to cut to the indispensable core of a major thinker's work, explicating, achieving an understanding, Trilling often pushing back at the text, viewing it as a locus of problematical energy."* No great surprise, then, that their writing styles also diverged. Trilling's prose weighed, qualified, probed, and coiled around ideas as if they were large amorphous limbs. Barzun's

*Jeffrey Hart, "Jacques Barzun at 100," *New Criterion,* November 2007.

was more of a means to an end. He wanted, as he acknowledged, "to compress great batches of fact and opinion into descriptions and conclusions that the reader of history could grasp," whereas his colleague "was bent on developing the large consequences of the often hidden relations and implications for life that he found in literature."

According to Barzun, Trilling would tell him: "Open it up—that sentence deserves a paragraph . . . that paragraph, a page." In turn, Barzun thought Trilling's style was marked by a tension "between the desire to show the complexity that thought must attain in order to do reality justice and the need for lucid simplifying which teaching undergraduates or reviewing books for general readers entails." He professed amazement at Trilling's ability to form a nuanced synthesis of literature, culture, politics, and psychology, but also regarded some of the essays as "visions" that "resembled in effect the rose window of a cathedral." Indeed, Trilling seemed so adept at creating a synthesis that Barzun occasionally wanted to shout: "Evidence, please!"

Trilling's prose may have been the more convoluted, but his career was certainly more straightforward. He wrote, lectured, served on committees, and attended parties. Barzun did likewise, but he also became a consultant to *Life* magazine, the literary critic for *Harper's,* a director of the Macmillan publishing company, a member of the Council on Foreign Relations, and a member or trustee of various boards and institutions, including the Boston Athenaeum, the Aspen Institute, and the *American Scholar.* He was twice president of the American Academy of Arts and Letters and from 1957 to 1967 served as provost of Columbia University. He also published some forty books, including *The House of Intellect* and *Berlioz and the Romantic Century,* along with countless reviews, articles, and essays. In June 1956 he showed up on the cover of *Time* magazine, looking a little like Gore Vidal.

Trilling was not nearly so worldly or prolific, but his books on Matthew Arnold, E. M. Forster, and the essays reprinted in *The Liberal Imagination, The Opposing Self,* and *Sincerity and Authenticity* made him in the eyes of many readers the most important critic of his day. Far more than Barzun, Trilling was seen as the critical voice of the generations that came of age during the 1940s and '50s. His writings affirmed correlations between moral concerns and imaginative artifice, between intellectual values and aesthetic taste. And together the two men proceeded to carve out a new discipline in American education: cultural criticism.

As I wrote elsewhere: "They broadened the critical spectrum to include the biographical and social conditions attending the creation of any cultural artifact." Not for them the tyrannous pieties of the Marxists, the New Critics, or the Russian formalists. Instead they believed in the essential messiness of culture, in the give-and-take between art and society. In his essay "On the Teaching of Modern Literature," Trilling proposed that modernist literature surpassed earlier works in power and substance because of its perilous relation to, and rejection of, the society that summoned it. In effect, the energies that thrust modernist literature into existence are antithetical to the taming or the teaching of it.

Although he never hid his interest in the class struggle or the Freudian currents disrupting both society and ourselves, the picture of Trilling that emerged in the decades after his death was the Trilling of the moral imagination, the Trilling for whom literature "is the human activity that takes the fullest and most precise account of variousness, possibility, complexity, and difficulty." How could we not admire his intelligence, sensitivity, and psychological insight? We thought him the most judicious of men and felt that, at their core, his essays were an incarnation of literature itself.

But we were missing something: mainly, a darker, decidedly less sanguine Trilling. As Edward Mendelson—appropriately the Lionel Trilling Professor in the Humanities at Columbia—recently wrote, Trilling's "strength as a critic was not the product of the sober urbanity for which he was celebrated, but his inward experience of the unrepressed, anarchic daemonic energy that, he imagined, set modern art in opposition to modern culture and made the modern artist a dangerous and destructive force." And Trilling wanted to be dangerous, he wanted to be a novelist like D. H. Lawrence or Hemingway, men who fought and loved in the "real" world.

It's Trilling's journals that have prompted a new set of speculations about his character. Citing from the journals as well as from Diana Trilling's 1993 memoir, *The Beginning of the Journey,* Louis Menand painted in 2008 a different picture of Trilling:

> He hated being regarded as a paragon of anything . . . he did not consider himself a scholar. . . . He did not consider himself a critic, either, and was surprised when he heard himself referred to as one. His ambition was to be a great novelist; he regarded his criticism as "an afterthought." He disliked Columbia; he disliked most of his colleagues; he disliked teaching graduate students. . . . He was depressive, he had writer's block, and he drank too much. He did not even like his first name. He wished that he had been called John or Jack.*

Menand has a basis for his claims but overstates and does so, one can't help feeling, for effect. Trilling, famously, had other detractors, people closer to home. Diana's memoir identifies her as the creator of Jack's prose style and often portrays her

*The *New Yorker,* September 22, 2008.

husband in an unfavorable light. Even more damaging was Trilling's son James's 1999 article in the *American Scholar,* "My Father and the Weak-Eyed Devils," with its explicit reference to Trilling's attention deficit disorder: "During his entire career as an interpreter of literature, I doubt that my father ever solved a problem, in the sense of marshaling evidence to prove or disprove a theory. On the contrary, he built his career on the mistrust of certainties and was rarely content with a simple answer when a complex one could be found. . . . Of all 'simple' solutions he mistrusted happiness the most."

There's no point in arguing with family members' feelings about each other; they're seeing the person they live with, not the one who thinks and writes. Trilling was, indeed, a neurotic, as was his wife; and he *was* haunted by his perceived failure to be another Hemingway, and perhaps haunted by his wife as well. As for the journals, yes, they can read like an indictment, especially if one is inclined, like Menand, to take Trilling down a peg.

From 1950:

> I am ashamed of being in a university. I have one of the great reputations in the academic world. This thought makes me retch.

> My intense disgust with my official and public self, my growing desire to repudiate it.

A decade later he writes about a faculty cocktail party:

> The doggy quality of its members—the sick self-consciousness, the bad quality, the trashiness, the sad discrepancy between them and their subject.

Nor had his disposition improved years later, when he attended an event for Jacques Barzun at the Century Club:

> Such sadness as I felt!—How empty the occasion. The sense that these were not entire people, were simulacra of the way people are expected to be—and that this was the peculiar Columbia characteristic, this mild, virtuous two-dimensionality.

And finally:

> My being a professor and a much respected and even admired one is a great hoax. . . . Suppose I were to dare to believe that one could be a professor and a man! and a writer!

A professor . . . a man . . . a writer—an unattainable trifecta, apparently.

So what do we make of this miserable, disaffected man who wanted to be a novelist but had to settle for being a critic? Do we pity him? Do we think how well he managed despite his depression and attention deficit disorder? I suggest we do neither. Journal entries jotted down late at night in the grip of loneliness or melancholy are always suspect. Anger, despair, frustration, disappointment, often fuel a writer's life, and some writers reach for their journals the way that other men reach for their bottles. Maybe what Trilling wrote was true, but it wasn't the whole truth, and it wasn't what he felt every minute of every day. As Rebecca West wisely observed: "Everyone realizes that one can believe little of what people say about each other. But it is not so widely realized that even less can one trust what people say about themselves."

If Trilling had been an insecure, self-obsessed, miserable human being suffering from ADD and depression, could he, even with his wife's help, have written so many essays and books, especially the lighthearted pieces he contributed to the book club's magazines? Perhaps. But one thing certain is that such a person would not have been Jacques Barzun's closest friend, and Barzun would never have addressed him in the following manner:

> Dear, darling Lionel, you are an ass! You send me a wonderful paper and ask me in the tones of a timid child whether you should put it away and think no more about it. If you do not publish it, at once, and send me a copy for frequent consultation, I shall haunt you.

What, then, was the basis of their friendship? In part, it was their differences, which, having initially kept them at arm's length, gradually drew them closer. Quite likely the Queens-bred Trilling was drawn to Barzun's elegance and quiet authority, while Barzun was stirred by Trilling's melancholic cast of mind, which, in some respects, mirrored the pessimism that occasionally surfaced in Barzun's own work and conversation. Ultimately, however, it was their attachment to ideals that bonded them. Both men believed in the restorative power of literature, and the colloquium and seminar became a means to tap into that power. As Trilling wrote of their shared enterprise: "If, it is of the essence of modern artistic culture that it confirms and expresses the idea of the pointlessness of existence, it might be said of the Colloquium that it was of its nature inhospitable to modern artistic culture. The books we read were massed against it—they were nothing if not affirmative."

Literature, then, was salvation, although in Trilling's case it came at a cost. To read his journals and notes, one gets the feeling that an appreciation of modernism aligns with a fatalistic view of existence. Trilling seemed disturbed to be alive; the world chafed at him; and its meaning, by eluding him, helped to define his approach to books. To escape, he sometimes went fishing. Barzun, who saw no point at all in baiting a hook, lived in the world that did not require a profound explanation for its existence, and for whatever reasons he seemed devoid of the neuroses, vanities, and jagged edges typical of so many of the New York Intellectuals.

Nonetheless, they subtly and profoundly influenced each other. Barzun's writings deepened owing to Trilling's exhortations to "open it up." And Trilling, I think, was emboldened by Barzun to see literature as a continuity animated by scientific progress, philosophical swervings, and societal changes. In his essay "Mind in the Modern World," Trilling noted that it was "the intense imagining of the past" that gave "impetus to all the shaping minds of the eighteenth and nineteenth centuries." It was precisely such historical awareness, he reasoned, that enabled Voltaire, Diderot, Rousseau, Jefferson, Goethe, Hegel, Darwin, Marx, and Freud to write so provocatively. Without such a commitment to history, he worried that our own writers would produce less original, less prophetic works.

Although Trilling's writings did not aspire to Barzun's thesaurus-like technique of discovering the synonyms and antonyms of various cultural periods, they had their own famous complexity. But whereas Barzun seemed energized by complexity and sought to put events in order, Trilling, if not weighed down by complexity, was obsessed by the desire to explore every aspect of it—which is a far cry from his son's unsavory characterization. A more accurate description of Trilling's approach to literature was offered by Irving Howe: Trilling "would circle a work with his fond, nervous wariness, as if in the presence of some force, some living energy, which could not always be kept under proper control." And this "nervous wariness," we might add, extended into his own life. Life was, to put it gently, tough sledding for Trilling. Barzun, on the other hand, drove the sled.

So am I making a case that opposites attract? Up to a point. Friendship is both constitutive and variable, and a friendship between minds that view the world differently but with equal force isn't unusual. It's the quality of mind that matters, not the qualities it sees in the world. And Barzun and Trilling shared a particular sensibility—mainly, a suspicion of ideologies and a commitment to the Arnoldian tenet that literature is a criticism of life. More than this, both men kept returning to the idea of something elemental and mysterious in great works of art, something that transcends the formal artifice of poems and novels. Call it a feeling for the primitive, which in Trilling's words was "of the highest value to the literary artist."

Although Menand wants us to remember the Trilling who felt thwarted emotionally, sexually, and artistically, who felt himself pulled between the strictures of civilization and the terrible force of instinct, it bears remembering that a close reading of poems and novels has its own interior logic: We read in order to appreciate what we've read before. And because Trilling *was* moved by poetry and fiction, because he was so open to the possibilities in literature, we have to take his own self-abasement with a grain of salt. His love of books could not be divorced from the very thing that repelled him about his own life, and it was this conflation that give his criticism its profound and discursive edge.

Barzun, too, was a complicated, if less conflicted, reader. Although he seemed the perfect embodiment of the mandarin scholar, he too was drawn to raw emotion. It was Berlioz, not Bach, to whom he gravitated. Like William James, his favorite philosopher, he believed that feelings are at the root of philosophy and art, and though his prose does not generate much heat, we find in it paeans to pure feeling: It is "the vulgarity of mankind," Barzun observed, that is "not only a source of art but the ultimate one." And: "Reading history remakes the mind by feeding primitive pleasure in story."

When I first came to know Barzun in the early 1970s, I would sometimes visit him in Low Memorial Library to talk about the books I was reading. One time I mentioned something by

Dostoevsky, and Barzun sat up and said, "The first time I read Dostoevsky, I felt like a savage seeing the sunrise." And I remember thinking skeptically, "Yeah, right!" The thought seemed antithetical to the dignified-looking man who uttered it. Or perhaps I, being twenty-two, simply couldn't imagine someone forty years older experiencing such a powerful emotion.

I also mistrusted, on another occasion, Barzun's admission that he suffered from a lack of vitality. Was it feasible that a man of his prodigious learning, uncommon industriousness, and various social and administrative duties lacked vitality? A deficiency which, he said, prevented him from doing more. The thought seemed preposterous, and I put it out of my mind. But now, five years after his death, I wonder if it wasn't this perceived deprivation that drew him to the likes of Berlioz and Byron—just as Trilling's sense of *his* shortcomings urged him toward Hemingway and Lawrence—writers who supposedly had *lived*.

Although I don't believe that either man spoke of his innermost fears and desires to the other, perhaps they recognized a kindred failure of the spirit. Could that have been the emotional substrata of their improbable friendship? It's hard to say. What I can say is that they wanted to see each other in the best possible light, a light afforded them by a colloquium, a graduate seminar, and a book club that lasted eleven years. And though Trilling eventually drew away as his depression deepened, I don't think he regretted a day of his friendship with Barzun.

Literature may have brought them together, but it wasn't what cemented their friendship. It was the pleasure they took in each other's company and in their awareness that art offers the most raw as well as the most refined figurations of reality. They understood that life and literature are complicated—a complication that requires thinking, and thinking, in its way, involves energy—and it was *this* energy, the charged thoughts that flowed between them, that accommodated their differences and made their friendship a deep and lasting one.

Originally published in the *Chronicle of Higher Education,* February 5, 2018. This essay is adapted from the 2016 Flora Levy Lecture, sponsored by the Department of English at the University of Louisiana.

Drawing America on Deadline

When I was much younger and didn't want to appear ignorant, I spent a fair amount of time in museums. I grew up in New York and could take a bus or train to the Metropolitan Museum of Art, the Museum of Modern Art, the Whitney, the Guggenheim, the Frick, and half a dozen others. In those days, the museums were free or cost little more than a dollar or two. Later, in my middle age, I visited museums in other cities both here and abroad, as well as various galleries in Manhattan. Nonetheless, I don't mind acknowledging that I cannot distinguish a great painting from a good one. Although I am amazed by the works of Velázquez, El Greco, Vermeer, and Van Gogh, I suspect that I admire them partially because they've been vetted by people whose opinions I respect. I don't doubt that Caravaggio's *The Calling of Saint Matthew* is a wonderful painting, but I'd be hard-pressed to say why it's better than some of his lesser-known work. This lack of discernment is, I've come to believe, almost a biological deficit: I simply don't have an eye for art.

As someone incapable of drawing a tree or a telephone pole, I find even an amateur portraitist, the ones hired at children's parties, a genius with pen and pencil. I don't know what goes into a painting or how the hand can represent what the eye sees. And when what is being depicted has nothing to do with how things really look, I have nothing to judge by. I sense rather than know that Picasso, Matisse, and Braque were geniuses, but art after

1960 is a blessèd mystery. Aside from Jackson Pollack, Mondrian, Munch, Hopper, and one or two others, I can drum up no interest in it. Lichtenstein is fun and Warhol is superficially interesting, but Rothko, De Kooning, Jasper Johns, and Reinhardt do not entrance me. I understand that abstract expressionism is about color and depth and the synesthesia of silence, sound, and motion, but it's not art I want to spend time with. Apparently, I am a man without visual qualities.

This isn't false modesty; it's simply a fact. Given that knowledgeable critics praise a great deal of abstract and postmodern art, I can only conclude the fault lies with me. And I accept this precisely because I am not modest. I believe I have a firm foundation in the slowly disappearing liberal arts, and I have no reservations about expressing opinions on literary and philosophical matters. To paraphrase a sly villain, I am nothing if not critical. And though I'm pretty sure that painters as different as Thomas Kinkade and Damien Hirst produce little of painterly or intellectual value, I can't take a scalpel to their work the way I can to a mediocre poem or overbaked novel.

If this failing has an upside, it's that it leaves me free to like what I like without guilt. And what I happen to like is illustration art, which by definition is any commissioned work put to use by another medium, be it books, calendars, or magazines. In a sense, illustration art goes back to the days when an artist was summoned by a prospective employer and told what to draw, paint, or sculpt. If not for Pope Julius II, a certain chapel ceiling in Rome might be bare. Perhaps the American muralist and art critic Kenyon Cox said it best: "Michael Angelo and Veronese were the two greatest illustrators who ever lived."

Maybe because the stakes are low or because I don't know any better, I get a kick out of old magazine covers, posters, book illustrations, and billboards. Of course, when I was coming of age in the 1960s and '70s, illustration art was decidedly not Art. Part of its appeal, in fact, lay in its substandard technique and kitschiness. Because it wasn't done to sell itself but rather to call attention to a product, it was considered a means to an end. Serious artists did not, so it was said, undertake to paint a canvas whose image would be used as an advertisement for a soap, a movie, or a story. Nonetheless, Cox's point does blur the line between illustration and artwork.

Surely art does not end where illustration begins. Handwritten medieval books containing illuminated pages of gold leaf, vellum, and silverpoint depicting religious scenes cannot be dismissed as mere decoration. The same can be said, of course, for any number of etchings, engravings, and lithographs. Indeed, as long as printers found it difficult to reproduce original works, illustrations were undertaken by recognized artists whose efforts were prized by both critics and collectors. A short list includes Honoré Daumier, George Catlin, John James Audubon, George and Charles Cruikshank, John Tenniel, Aubrey Beardsley, Toulouse-Lautrec, and Hablot Knight Browne, who illustrated Dickens's novels. Why then claim a difference in intent between a pen-and-ink drawing found in an 1890 novel and the woodcuts used to illustrate gorgeous block books made in 1490?

Toward the latter part of the mid-nineteenth century a conflation of events both facilitated the illustrator's art and ultimately tarred it with the brush of commerce. Advances in photography, in particular the halftone, made works in gouache or oil easier to represent on a photographic plate, making them more accessible as both covers for magazines and pictures in books. Improvements in mechanical presses, the growth of publishing, and the increasing number of magazines (in 1800 there were around one hundred magazines in the United States; by 1900 there were around 3,500) combined to create a thriving marketplace for illustrations.

And so the history of illustration art became entwined with the history of magazine publishing.

According to a 1900 census, some magazines had circulations in the hundreds of thousands and were commonplace in homes throughout the country. This was largely the result of population growth (by 1900 the total population had reached seventy-six million, more than three times what it had been in 1850). There was greater literacy, more disposable income, a decline in production costs matched by improvements in distribution, and a greater availability of paper. And then, of course, there was the rise of print advertising.*

In 1897 *Scribner's* became the first magazine to run ads, thereby encouraging the manufacturers who made soap, tools, and towels to hire artists to depict people enjoying their products. Soon the *Saturday Evening Post, Harper's, Collier's, McCall's,* and *Harper's Bazaar* began employing these same artists to create covers and advertisements that drew attention to their *own* magazines. Although intended for popular consumption, illustration art between 1880 and 1920 was still highly regarded, and such notable illustrators as Howard Pyle (often referred to as the father of illustration art in America), Maxfield Parrish, N. C. Wyeth, Howard Chandler Christy, and Jessie Wilcox Smith were celebrities in their own right and often called upon to function as arbiters of taste. Christy, the creator of the "Christy Girl," was the sole judge of the first Miss America Pageant in 1921, and was joined the following year by James Montgomery Flagg, Coles Phillips, and Norman Rockwell. Nor did they work cheap. Charles Dana Gibson, creator of the "Gibson Girl" was paid $100,000 to produce a hundred works over four years for *Collier's;* another illustrator, Howard Fisher, earned $3,000 for his *Cosmopolitan* covers.

---

* See *Historical Statistics of the United States,* 1975.

But even as illustrators were enjoying success, the golden age of illustration art was drawing to a close. Part of the blame was attributable to the excitement attending modernist art with its newfound political and philosophical implications. Surrealism, Dadaism, and cubism were about more than painting; they said something about how Art progresses and how certain shapes and colors reflect and illuminate the psyche. How could mere illustrations compete with canvases that proffered symbolic and psychological truths? So even as illustrators prospered, their craft became lowered in the public's esteem.

Illustration art gradually became a pejorative term associated with crass commercialism, and by the time Edward Hopper took to illustrating for a quick buck in the early 1900s, he was swift to dismiss his own efforts. Making matters worse was the rise of a new kind of illustration. After World War I, a proliferation of magazines flooded the market, catering to less sophisticated tastes, and their covers welcomed a poorer quality of illustration, ranging from the fantastic to the foolish. These magazines, known as "the pulps," were printed on paper of the lowest quality and soon featured sensationalist fiction and even more unlikely ads. The writing was often simplistic, hackneyed, and derivative, and the artwork was meant to catch the eye by poking it with a gun barrel or a breast.

The first pulp magazine, the *Argosy,* appeared in 1896, followed by *Popular Magazine, Black Mask, Dime Detective, Flying Aces, Horror Stories, Amazing Stories, Marvel Tales, Oriental Stories, Planet Stories, Spicy Detective,* and the like. Perhaps the historical watershed where the pulps are concerned was *All-Story*'s publication in 1912 of the first of two serialized novels by Edgar Rice Burroughs: *Under the Moons of Mars,* and *Tarzan of the Apes, A Romance of the Jungle,* whose cover by Clinton Pettee may be the most valuable pulp magazine cover in existence. One day the figure of Tarzan had not existed and then one day, thanks to

Pettee, there he was in all his lean, muscled splendor. Pettee, who also drew for the *Literary Digest, Scientific American,* and *Motor Age* and illustrated such novels as *Darkness and Dawn* (1914), *The Unseen Hand* (1918), and *The Other Side of the Wall* (1919), was followed by N. C. Wyeth and J. Allen St. John as a Tarzan artist.

While neither a Tolstoy nor a Titian ever dropped work off at a pulp magazine, some of the better ones managed to publish stories by Dashiell Hammett, Cornell Woolrich, Raymond Chandler, H. P. Lovecraft, Ray Bradbury, and a sixteen-year-old novice by the name of Thomas Lanier Williams. As for the men and women who created the cover art, none became household names, yet most were generally better trained than the writers whose work they illustrated. The artists most in demand—Wyeth, Rudolph Belarski, H. J. Ward, Rafael de Soto, Henry Reuterdahl, John Held, Frank Paul, Virgil Finlay, and J. Allen St. John—were but a fraction of the men who drew for the pulps. Most didn't bother to sign their paintings, and the covers often bore no attribution. They, like the hack writers, worked on assignment. Told what kind of story they'd be illustrating, they might spend five or six days painting. They painted on canvas or, when that was too expensive, on board, and used oil or gouache. Artists were generally paid between fifty and one hundred dollars per assignment, and once the work was finished, delivered, and photographed, it was usually forgotten.

There were far fewer women illustrators for all the obvious reasons: Dorothy Flack, Thelma Gooch, Margery Stocking Hart, and Alice Kirkpatrick among them. The best known and currently the one most popular with collectors is Margaret Brundage, the main artist for *Weird Tales,* who often worked with pastel on illustration board. Between 1933 and 1945 she produced sixty-six paintings for the magazine. "Art deco dynamite" is how one collector described them. There's some truth to this. Brundage's flowing soft-bodied women, all but nude, signal both sexual languor and sexual appetite. Her covers proffer a genteel lesbianism for those who like the female form idealized, although a few featured scenes of women trapped in sexually vulnerable situations. One cover showing a woman whipping another was banned in Canada.

The pulps were never meant to last and pretty much died out in the 1950s, outmuscled by comic books and paperbacks. Of the approximate fifty thousand paintings that served as models for the covers, most were tossed out, left to rot in publishers' storerooms, or sold off as junk. Fewer than three thousand are known to exist today. but those that managed to survive eventually found respectability in the hands of collectors. The most painterly of the illustrators and one of the most sought after remains J. Allen St. John, who had studied in New York and Paris and later taught at the American Academy of Art in Chicago. He provided illustrations for books and slick magazines, and his "Golden Bowl" cover for the April 1933 *Weird Tales* is famous in the annals of pulp.

Educated readers naturally turned up their noses at the pulps, though Wittgenstein evidently was enamored of Street & Smith's *Detective Story Magazine.* The "slicks"—*Harper's,* the *Atlantic, Scribner's, Collier's,* and the *Saturday Evening Post*—were what the better writers and illustrators aspired to. The cover of *Life* magazine was a coup, as was the *Saturday Evening Post.* But *Life* as a weekly was gone by 1973, and the *Post*'s run ended in 1969. Illustrators still found work creating drawings and paintings for posters, books, calendars, and various catalogs, but compared to abstract expressionism or the ironic self-awareness of Pop Art, even the best illustrations seemed hopelessly middlebrow.

But fashion, as we know, rides a pendulum, and by the 1980s illustration art had recovered a measure of respectability, aided in part by the tremendously popular 1976 "Two Hundred Years of American Illustration," sponsored by the New York Historical

Society.* Somewhat belatedly, in 1989, Sotheby's gave its imprimatur to illustration art by putting a Rockwell painting on the cover of its *American Painting Sale Catalog.* The following year the Norman Rockwell exhibit at the Palazzo delle Esposizioni museum in Rome drew twice as many people as did the Rubens show that preceded it; and in 1992 another Rockwell show, this one at Toyko's Isetan department store, was attended by over 300,000 people in six weeks, easily outdistancing a nearly contemporaneous Picasso exhibit.

Some of this attention is attributable to a fascination with *les choses américaines.* Maxwell Parrish's dreamlike waifs reclining against cobalt blue backdrops notwithstanding, the vast majority of illustrators took for their subject American life in the cities and on the Great Plains. Whether they captured reality or only produced idealized and sentimentalized versions of it remains a tricky question. Nature has a way of imitating illustration art as well as it does fine art. Whatever the case, J. C. Leyendecker's "Arrow Collar Man," James Montgomery Flagg's "I Want You" recruitment poster, and almost all of Norman Rockwell's oeuvre not only presented America to the world but became part of it as well.

Prices naturally reflected this newfound interest in illustration art. And while there is no shortage of available works, probably two-thirds of the original paintings, according to Roger Reed of Illustration House in New York City, have been destroyed. "Once a reproduction was done," Reed notes, "there was no further need for the paintings, so publishers often threw them away." What remains, however, sells. A Gibson pen-and-ink drawing commands tens of thousands of dollars. J. C. Leyendecker's *Arrow Collar Couple* fetched almost $40,000 at a 1986 Guernsey's auction, and another Leyendecker, *The Lady and Her Motorcar,* was sold

---

*The 1968 Norman Rockwell exhibit mounted by the Brooklyn Museum of Art certainly advanced Rockwell's reputation, but it's hard to know if other illustrators benefited.

privately for $75,000. Maxfield Parrish's paintings are often valued in the millions. Indeed, the blue-chip illustrators—Rockwell, Pyle, Wyeth, Christy—now command higher prices than some of the Old Masters. In 1999 George Bellows's *Polo Crowd* sold for $27.7 million, and in 2003 Norman Rockwell's *Saying Grace,* which appeared on the cover of the *Saturday Evening Post* in 1951 and for which he was paid $3,500, fetched $46 million at a Sotheby's auction. Even the colorful and loony paintings that became the covers of the pulps now command good and even exorbitant prices. In 2019 Frank R. Paul's *The Moon Conquerors* (*Science Wonder Quarterly,* Winter 1930) went for $87,500, thanks to bids from twenty-eight collectors.

The price of pulp art was considerably ramped up in the 1980s by the collector Robert Lesser, whose three-room apartment in New York was literally covered from floor to ceiling with nearly two hundred original paintings. Lesser's collection became part of the exhibits at the Brooklyn Museum (2003), the Society of Illustrators (2012), and the Union Club (2019), and now resides with the New Britain Museum of American Art in Connecticut. No one, I think, would be more surprised by this acclaim than the painters themselves. Indeed, the question of how good the paintings are may not really matter. The best illustrators took their work seriously and acquitted themselves honorably. One might tentatively compare them to the songwriters of Tin Pan Ally or to those who composed tunes for the old-fashioned musical revues. It ain't Bach, but if it's Jerome Kern it's good enough for me. There's a place for both Sir Walter Scott's *Lady of the Lake* and Raymond Chandler's *Lady in the Lake.* Does it need saying that each deserves an illustrator equal to the task?

Adapted from *Art & Antiques,* March 1994 and Summer 1994.

The Tan Tarzan of Thump

JOE LOUIS AND WHITE AMERICA

On the night of June 22, 1937, in Chicago's Comiskey Park, a shy, inarticulate twenty-three-year-old Black man knocked out James J. Braddock to become heavyweight champion of the world. Although not everyone had predicted the outcome, most people by then had heard of Joe Louis Barrow. From 1934, when he turned professional, to 1936, more had been written about Louis, estimated Damon Runyon, than about any living man, with the exception of Charles Lindbergh. Although Louis would always remain good copy, the significance of his early celebrity would pall during the sixties when Black athletes and politicians were routinely making headlines. But in the thirties, intensive coverage of a Black man was without precedent, and according to Chris Mead's *Champion: Joe Louis, Black Hero in White America,* the media's representation of Joe Louis both reflected and altered the face of prejudice in American society.

Those born after 1945 won't remember Louis's preeminence in the ring or enormous popularity outside it. He reigned from 1937 to 1951, dominating his profession as no boxer has done before or since, becoming, in the process, one of the most recognizable men in America. The only other nationally known Black man at the time was Father Divine, the entrepreneurial evangelist, whom the white press treated with thinly veiled contempt. There were notable Blacks before Louis, of course: intellectuals like W. E. B. Du Bois and A. Philip Randolph; entertainers like Bill "Bojangles"

Robinson, Louis Armstrong, and Paul Robeson, who occasionally made the back pages of major newspapers; and there were athletes like Jesse Owens, whose magnificent performance during the 1936 Olympic Games caused more than a ripple of excitement on the sports pages. But, by and large, white people weren't interested in hearing about Blacks.

Louis was the exception, in part because heavyweight boxers have always enjoyed a disproportionate fame, but primarily because journalists fastened onto Louis and created a public demand for news about him. The inevitable irony is that Louis himself became something of a cipher, buried under sheets of newsprint. Nor was this really unintended. Louis's wily managers realized that in order for him to get a title fight, he had to be seen as an inoffensive, stereotypical Negro. In 1934 the public was not exactly clamoring for a Black heavyweight. The memory of Arthur (Jack) Johnson, the first Black man to hold the title (1908–15) under Marquess of Queensberry rules, still rankled in whites. Johnson had been a world beater, also a world baiter, strutting his stuff in and out of the ring: boozing, boasting, openly consorting with prostitutes, and even marrying a white woman. Blacks may have exulted when Johnson decked a white opponent, but they did so at their peril; at least eight Black men were killed in rioting after the Johnson-Jeffries fight in 1910.

Not every Black fighter, however, automatically brought out the white sheets. A number of fine boxers, including Sam McVey, Joe Jeannette, Sam Langford (the "Boston Tar Baby"), and the great West Indian fighter Peter Jackson, whom John L. Sullivan assiduously ducked, fought in relative obscurity around the beginning of the century. Johnson fanned racial hatred not only because he was Black but because he was boorish, someone in fact whom many Blacks disliked; and while his victories gave them a secret frisson of satisfaction, his bumptiousness made it extremely difficult for Black fighters who came after him. Of the forty-three men Louis fought before 1945, only one had been Black. Louis's first step to the championship was around the shadow cast by Johnson. His ambition was served by two factors: the scarcity of good heavyweights after Gene Tunney retired in 1928 and a shrewd public relations campaign centered around seven rules drawn up by his managers and approvingly run by the white press.

1. He was never to have his picture taken along with a white woman.
2. He was never to go to a nightclub alone.
3. There would be no soft fights.
4. There would be no fixed fights.
5. He was never to gloat over a fallen opponent.
6. He was to keep a "dead pan" in front of the camera.
7. He was to live and fight clean.

The official image of the well-behaved Negro stayed with Louis the rest of his life, despite certain misadventures. When he was coming up, whites were only too happy to see him as a good-natured darky who knew how to punch. The most fair-minded sportswriters regularly alluded to his color, and even those who genuinely liked him coined patronizing, alliterative epithets. Louis was the "Brown Bomber," of course, but he was also the "Sepia Slugger," "Tan Tornado," "Sable Cyclone," "Dark Dynamiter," "Mocha Mauler," "Coffee-Colored Kayo King," and, my favorite, the "Tan Tarzan of Thump."

In many of the first press releases, Louis was the stereotyped distillation of his race: a hulking Negro who liked his jazz and fried chicken and who fought with a native—i.e., nonwhite—savagery. In the ring, he was the jungle killer who stalked his prey without mercy; outside of it, he wouldn't do a lick of work if he could help it. The liberal Paul Gallico of the *New York Daily News* reflected an unconscious, most insidious kind of prejudice when he described Louis as "a truly savage person, a man on whom civilization rested no more securely than a shawl thrown over one's shoulders." Racial misconceptions also extended to Louis's boxing skills. Bill Corum of the *New York Journal* voiced a typical sentiment before the second Schmeling fight: "There are certain gifts that the Negro race, as a race, and Louis, as an individual, have as a heritage. The ability carefully to work out a methodical plan and adhere to it, is not among them."

The truth is, Louis was the most methodical of fighters, who would, as A. J. Liebling might say, always interpret his opponents in interesting ways. Still, many reporters seemed oblivious to his conditioning and discipline in the ring. After the first Schmeling fight, even his jab became suspect to one boxing maven. Louis, of course, had the sweetest jab of any heavyweight until Muhammad Ali came along. As for his heralded savagery, it existed only in print. True brawlers, such as Henry Armstrong, Jack Dempsey, and Harry Greb, made Louis seem like a study in patience. Then again, not every observer let prejudice tamper with the evidence. Jonathan Mitchell of the *New Republic* wrote that Louis "reeks of study, practice, study. He suggests a gorilla or a jungle lion as much as would an assistant professor at the Massachusetts Institute of Technology."

If Louis had only inspired contradictory accounts of his skills based on racial bias, Chris Mead would have had the makings of an interesting monograph. But Louis was to become more than fodder for sportswriters. After his loss to the German champion Max Schmeling in 1936, he unwittingly stepped into the arena of international politics. Hitler, who had prudently taken no notice of that fight, now crowed over Schmeling's unassailable Aryan superiority. In short order, the Reich commissioned a film, *Max Schmeling's Victory—a German Victory,* which played to full houses across Germany.

By the rematch two years later, chauvinistic hysteria, fueled by the growing hostility between the two nations, saturated the pre-fight publicity. Casting the gentlemanly Schmeling as the villain, the press presented Louis as a product of America's progressive social policies. With Germany a patently racist state, America had suddenly become an open and tolerant society. And when Louis and Schmeling stepped into the ring in Yankee Stadium on June 22, 1938, democracy and fascism came out slugging at the bell. The fight was over in two minutes and four seconds, time enough for Louis to rewrite the role the media had cast him in.

Although some journalists continued to quote Louis in dialect, exaggerating his eating and sleeping habits, most came around to the idea that focusing on color was inappropriate in Louis's case. Not only had he bested the Nazis' champion and enlisted as soon as war broke out, but his natural reserve and quiet deportment won their respect. The postwar Joe Louis was not the instinctively brutal fighter of the thirties; instead he had become, in Jimmy Cannon's famous words, "a credit to his race—the human race." And as he got older and slower and his fights became progressively more difficult, the press sang his praises, acknowledging his courage as well as his fading skills.

It was during this period, 1939–51, argues Mead, that Louis induced a new awareness of race in America. Because many whites, urged on by the media, were exhorting Louis to beat all comers, Black or white, they had to rethink long-held convictions about Negroes. Black observers, too, now came to regard Louis as a bellwether for racial progress. "Give [whites] the impression that Negro is a synonym for Joe Louis," wrote Theophilus Lewis in the *New York Amsterdam News,* "and race relations will change for the better."

A happy thought certainly, but did it square with the facts? How do we measure Louis's influence? I don't mean his influence in opening doors for Blacks; Louis was probably the first Black man to show both races that Black advancement in sports was inevitable. Without his example, the color line in baseball might not have been broken as early as 1947, and white reporters might have overstated Jackie Robinson's catlike agility and naturally aggressive, or nonwhite, style of base running. But what about the torrents of abuse Robinson encountered from fans and players alike? Other Black personalities fared no better. In 1951 Josephine Baker was denied service at New York's Stork Club, a favorite haunt of Joe Louis.

In fact, Louis was not synonymous with Negro in the minds of most whites. He was a good Negro, not a representative one. A white man could cheer for Louis while barring Black children from public schools. Nevertheless, Mead contends that the sympathetic press coverage Louis received after the war must have had a beneficial effect on race relations. This is rather difficult to prove. What, after all, is the correlation between the media's reporting of an event and the public's views on that event? Does the media speak for the majority of Americans, or is it, as many people now maintain, a minority liberal organ? Louis may have swayed some whites to reassess their feelings about Negroes, but surely prejudice runs too deep for any one individual to excavate it on his own.

Louis's real contribution may, indeed, be viewed in a different light entirely. If whites didn't accept Blacks with more alacrity because of Louis, Blacks accepted white authority with less and less equanimity. Even though liberals made it a point of honor to ignore Louis's race, Blacks never forgot it. Louis was a Black man beating white men at a game of skill and strength, and to Blacks Louis was always a Black hero before he was an American hero. There is a further irony in this. As Mead reminds us, many middle-class Blacks were ambivalent about the esteem in which Louis was held. Here was an uneducated Negro, viewed by whites as the paradigm of his race, who obviously would not be commanding such respect if he were a scientist or businessman. Black newspapers such as the *Chicago Defender* and the *New York Amsterdam News* even ran articles downplaying Louis's role as a model for Blacks. Still, it had to be a curiously detached Black person who wasn't thrilled when Louis won and who didn't weep when Marciano finally put him down in 1951.

As if to atone for all the bad press they had given Louis, journalists in the fifties and sixties fell over themselves trying to excuse Louis's burgeoning paranoia, cocaine habit, and tax problems. While Louis was an admirable man in many respects—generous, hard-working, modest—he was also irresponsible with money and people, his wife for one. Yes, Joe had an eye for the ladies, and color didn't count. But if reporters ever got wind of Louis's philandering ways, they kept quiet about it. No "Brown Boffer," "Sepia Swinger," or "Tan Tomcat" sprang out from headlines. And when Louis ended up as a greeter at Caesars Palace in Las Vegas, the press decided that he had been dealt a bad hand by his country. Not so, says Mead. Louis liked being a greeter; he was comfortable with crowds and had come to expect their adulation. Also, he had always assumed he would be provided for. So the end of his career, much like the beginning, was a projection of the media's racial sensibilities.

I never saw Louis fight except on film, and I wasn't born until he was already a fixture in American life. I was too young really to appreciate the popularity that cut across lines of color and class, but Mead has convinced me. Louis's fabled "dignity," the word most often applied to him, is something not even A. J. Liebling was immune to, and Liebling had a built-in resistance to sham. Covering the second Sugar Ray Robinson–Randy Turpin fight in 1951, Liebling noted that when Louis, who was no longer champion, walked out on the field of the Polo Grounds, he received a bigger ovation than General MacArthur, who had preceded him.

"Louis looks like a champion and carries himself like a champion, and people will continue to call him champion as long as he lives."

In fact, it is only a small exaggeration to say that Louis was champion before he was anything else, having no other identity in the public's mind. Consequently, Mead's book is not meant as a biography but as a palimpsest of the public faces of Joe Louis, who at age twenty-three became a symbol of his race—a symbol whose subsequent metamorphosis would reflect both America's willingness and its incapacity to overcome a history of discrimination.

Although consistently illuminating in transcribing the prejudice that lay beneath the most "enlightened" print journalism of the past half century, *Champion* suffers on occasion from its author's zealousness. Banging away at Louis's carefully manicured public image, Mead finally had me reeling from the repetitions. He is best when commenting on the words of others but somewhat stodgy when reviewing the history of sports or boxing. Here, his prose could do with some punching up, as it were. But this does not detract from his considerable achievement. He has tackled an interesting subject and done it justice, telling us in the end more about ourselves than about a boxer by the name of Joe Louis.

When Joe Louis died on April 12, 1981, whites and Blacks alike mourned, though I think their grief, too, had a different hue. How Blacks felt, I would not want to say. For whites, Louis's death represented, I believe, a loss of innocence. He was the last Black man of prominence whom whites felt they could manipulate. Whatever the media's intentions, manipulate him they did. As Mead makes so very clear, journalists monitored, distorted, and disseminated Joe Louis until he finally disappeared up America's sanctimonious vision of itself.

Originally published in the *American Scholar,* Winter 1987.

The Day Muhammad Ali Punched Me

On June 4, 1991, at approximately 3:45 p.m., Muhammad Ali punched me in the face—not in the ring but on a Trailways bus cruising along Interstate 78—and I deserved it. I had boarded the bus earlier that day, in Manhattan, along with some fifteen journalists and photographers, plus members of Ali's entourage. We were headed toward Ali's old training camp in Deer Lake, Pennsylvania, about twenty-five miles from Reading. The sportswriters Dick Schaap, Sal Marchiano, Robert Lipsyte, and Ralph Wiley were along for the ride, as was the former heavyweight contender Earnie Shavers. I was there because I had reviewed Tom Hauser's oral biography of Ali, *Muhammad Ali: His Life and Times,* which had just been published and was the occasion for the press junket.

Ali was already on the bus when we clambered aboard. He looked large and heavy, in a tan safari jacket and pants, and greeted everyone with looks of delighted recognition. Seeing me, he just smiled and introduced himself. I'd never met Ali before and, frankly, I was stunned that he existed in three dimensions. Like Elvis or the Eiffel Tower, Ali seemed to belong to photographs, posters, and television screens.

An hour into the trip, everyone had settled in. Writers schmoozed or dozed. Ali slept, too, until Howard Bingham, his official photographer, tickled his ear with a piece of tissue. Ali woke up, glared around him, and put on a look of mock astonishment. A bit later, as I was nodding off, I heard a commotion behind me.

I turned and saw Ali's 250-pound frame sprawled across the lap of a dignified gray-haired man in a dark suit who was shouting, "Oh, oh, ohhh!" The man was Jeremiah Shabazz, a Muslim minister and not someone you'd tap on the shoulder much less collapse upon. But Shabazz, who traveled frequently with Ali, had been pinned by him on numerous planes, trains, and buses.

Ali's camp was a five-acre spread at the top of a steep hill, just off Highway 61. It consisted of a main building, a dozen log cabins, a small white mosque, and, of course, the boulders. Years earlier, Ali had painted the name Sonny Liston on a boulder that belonged to the property. People then began sending Ali giant rocks, and when each one arrived he assigned it a name. "Rocky Marciano" wasn't far from "Joe Louis," and a little distance away were "Jersey Joe Walcott" and "Archie Moore." The promoter Don King also had a boulder, which, according to Ali's cornerman, Wali (Blood) Muhammad, King had inscribed himself before hauling it up to the camp.

After lunch, Ali posed for photographs on top of "Sonny Liston." He looked tired, but mugged gamely for the cameras. Reporters asked the usual questions: How was his health? (Ali had been suffering from Parkinson's since the mid-eighties.) And what did he think of Evander Holyfield, the current champ? Ali was diplomatic. He also acknowledged his slurred speech. "I talk about boxing, I have trouble," he said, in his familiar feathery voice. "I talk about Allah and my voice gets better. Boxing was nothin'. Just a way to introduce me to the world. My real purpose is to carry the word of Allah."

A little later, Ali went to pray. I asked him if I could join him. He gave me a skeptical look, but nodded. The mosque was a small, single room, and I felt uncomfortable, standing just a few feet from Ali as he recited his prayers. Ali, however, didn't seem to mind, and when we left he gave me another look, as if to say, "Who are you, again?" It occurred to me only later that I had intruded on his privacy, but he gave no sign of it, and for whatever reason he acted friendlier toward me the rest of the day—until, that is, he slugged me.

It was Ralph Wiley who started the fracas. Wiley, who died unexpectedly, in 2004, at the age of fifty-two, was a much-liked writer and ESPN commentator. I had once favorably reviewed a book of his, and we had chatted amiably during the day and by chance found ourselves seated across the aisle from each other on the ride home. "Let me ask you something," Wiley said. "Who was the greatest Black fighter who ever lived?" He threw a meaningful glance at Ali, who was sitting directly behind me.

"The greatest Black fighter who ever lived," I mused aloud. "Hmm. Let's see, there was Jack Johnson."

"Johnson was something, all right," Wiley agreed.

"There's Henry Armstrong."

"Armstrong. Absolutely! Man held three titles back in the day."

"Then you have Sam Langford, Joe Louis, Sugar Ray Robin—"

"Yeah, O.K.," Wiley interrupted. "But if you had to choose *two* Black fighters who were the best ever and one is Sugar Ray Robinson, who'd the other one *have* to be?"

I could hear Ali shifting in his seat, leaning forward. I let the question hang a moment before I said, "Hell, that's easy. It'd have to be the man who beat Robinson for the title—Randy Turpin."

Ali's fist now crashed gently against my right cheek.

"Turpin!" Ali shouted hoarsely. "Turpin?"

Wiley began to hoot and slap his knee.

I rubbed my cheek, stood up, and turned toward Ali. "You ever touch me again and I'll clean your clock," I said evenly.

Wiley began to laugh harder as Ali stared at me, his eyes as open as the moment he'd heard that Liston wasn't coming out for the seventh round. "Clean my clock," he said wonderingly. "Clean my clock? I'm gonna clean *your* clock!" He made a fist, which looked very, very large.

"Randy Turpin!" Wiley shouted and pointed a finger at Ali. "Randy Turpin."

Ali chuckled and sat down.

The bus was quieter on the way home. The writers, as if by design, fell silent. Ali finally had some breathing room. He sat by himself and looked out the window. For maybe thirty minutes, it didn't matter that the most recognizable man in the world was sitting behind me. Then Jeremiah Shabazz began to shout, "Oh, oh, ohhh!"

At Fiftieth Street and Tenth Avenue, the camera crew and most of the journalists got off. The rest of us continued uptown, to 125th Street, to the home of a nonprofit called Our Children's Foundation. We entered a spacious room where some two hundred kids of all ages and races were waiting. Soon two lines of brightly dressed girls filed in from the wings and performed a "welcome dance" from Zaire, the country where, in 1974, Ali had wrested the heavyweight crown from George Foreman.

A teacher spoke briefly and presented Ali with an award. When Ali looked at the room full of expectant young faces, he seemed happy. "Everyone has a purpose," he said firmly. "Find out what your purpose is. Then work to achieve it." His voice sounded stronger than it had on the bus, and it certainly carried farther than that of the very nervous young man who recited a poem while its subject stood nearby: "You floated like a butterfly / You stung like a bee / We will always love you, Muhammad Ali."

Originally published in the *New Yorker,* June 7, 2016.

A Sentimental Education

THE BOOKS I KEEP

Books, books, books. I figure I own around 2,200 of them. Those that I haven't read, I probably won't, and those I have read I doubt I'll read again. In fact, perhaps only 1 percent matter to me as material objects, but they *do* matter. These twenty-odd books are neither rare nor valuable; some are even falling apart. Nonetheless, they have a place in my memory along the lines of tasting duck confit for the first time or coming nose to nose with a Siberian tiger in a gazebo. It makes no difference that their authors went on to write better books or no books at all. What's more, I wouldn't replace them with first editions or trade in an old softcover for a new hardback. Because then they wouldn't be *mine.* Most were acquired in secondhand bookstores or library sales; they didn't cost much then and probably, allowing for inflation, don't cost much now. You may own these books, too, but I'm willing to bet ten bucks and my bespoke shoes that you didn't read them precisely when and where I did.

Were you at 40 rue Blanche in Paris in the summer of 1970? Well, I was and so was a 1964 New Directions paperback edition of Borges's *Labyrinths: Selected Stories and Other Writings* with its now familiar muted black-and-gray cover photograph. How this book ended up in the darkly furnished apartment of a family friend, I can't say. But on a hot August day with rain pattering on the windows, I sat alone in a living room with too many chairs and lamps, immersed in stories whose narrative voice I had not encountered before: "I owe the discovery of Uqbar to the conjunction of a mirror and an encyclopedia. The mirror troubled the depths of a corridor in a country house on Gaona Street in Ramos Mejia." The scholarly tone, the amused hint of irony ("Mirrors and copulation are abominable, since they both multiply the numbers of men"), and the alternate reality of a world whose physical reality is disavowed seemed to me singular qualities absent from any previous fiction.

Although some early readers felt that Borges's stories were more about literature than credible examples of it, the critic George Steiner disagreed. "When he cites fictitious titles, imaginary cross-references, folios and writers that have never existed, Borges is simply regrouping counters of reality into the shape of possible other worlds." I generally don't write in my books, but my well-handled copy of Steiner's *Language and Silence* contains penciled brackets around various paragraphs and even one, on page 205, in (the horror!) red magic marker. Steiner was the first critic to make me see that art cannot redeem the world. His characterization of German officers listening to Schubert in the evening and going off in the morning to gas and burn human beings—now almost a trope regarding man's inhumanity to man—was a revelation to a young man whose grandparents might have been killed by those very officers.

Much of what Steiner later wrote seemed to me more intellectually elaborate than it needed to be, but *Language and Silence,* by which I mean my 1969 Picador/Penguin paperback, whose cover consists of a detail from Bosch's *Garden of Earthly Delights,* possesses for me the nostalgic quality of an old photograph showing someone who thought books held the key to wisdom. "Above all, a man's thought is his nostalgia," Camus observed, referring to our desire to be reconciled with the universe, which he believed was "the essential impulse of the human drama." My nostalgia is only marginally less grand. I want to be reconciled with the young man who studied philosophy and believed that Novalis's description of it as homesickness, the desire to be everywhere at home, was at the heart of his interest in literature.

There was a time when I couldn't bear to part with any book I cared about. Some because they represented a small financial sacrifice; others because they kept me company when I found myself alone in strange cities. I moved around a lot in my twenties and sometimes books were all I had. I remember apartments without a TV or radio or telephone. Telephone booths were my cell phone; libraries my Google. Books didn't so much sweep me away as keep me grounded. I burrowed into them, dug out a cozy pocket and lived there for a time. The few books I owned were stored in my parents' apartment in the Bronx, and the books I had read mostly came from the Fordham Public Library or libraries wherever I happened to land. And, of course, secondhand bookstores.

Although many of the bookstores along Fourth Avenue were gone by the time I began to visit Book Row in the late 1960s, a few remained, like the Academy Book Store on West Eighteenth Street, and whenever I found myself near Union Square, I made sure to walk a few blocks north. I also popped into the Argosy Book Store on East Fifty-Ninth Street, the Gotham Book Mart on East Forty-Sixth, and, of course, the Strand, which, truth be told, struck me the same way as a Wine Warehouse does today. I usually find what I'm looking for, but after fifteen minutes I'm ready to go.

One day, in 1986, in downtown Rochester, New York, I wandered by chance into a secondhand shop and gleefully made off with a pint-sized, reddish hardback of Arthur Conan Doyle's *The Croxley Master and Other Tales of the Ring and Camp.* There's no copyright date, but it was published by George H. Doran Company, which operated from 1908 to 1927, when it merged with Doubleday. Conan Doyle was a fan of the prize ring and wrote a half dozen stories about fisticuffs, including "The Bully of Brocas Court," which to my knowledge is the only story ever to feature a pugilistic ghost. You can buy a used copy for around five dollars on AbeBooks, but you'd have to pay me fifty times that for mine.

Today, the idea of halving my library doesn't bother me. If you're looking for a thousand books of poetry, fiction, history, biography, philosophy, and criticism, I'm the man to see. Nonetheless, there's that 1 percent that stays put. I doubt that I'll reach again for my green, case-bound 1961 Modern Library copy of *Ulysses,* but I don't see how I can let go of the amazement I felt the first time I read the damn thing. The same holds true for my New Directions sixth printing of Djuna Barnes's *Nightwood.* The novel's opening one-paragraph sentence doesn't seem as glorious as it did when I was twenty-four, but it did once and so the book stays. And like every other person who lives west of Broadway near Morningside Heights, I own the two-volume blue-and-beige Modern Library edition of Proust's *Remembrance of Things Past.* The first volume's copyright is 1934, while the second volume's is 1932, so it may not be a matched set, but I can handle that. And though C. K. Scott Moncrieff's translation has its well-documented flaws, I have no desire to measure it against more recent translations. Odd to think that these books were published just ten years after Proust's death in 1922, which means, of course, that his centennial *yahrzeit* has come and gone.

"My great adventure is really Proust. Well—what remains to be written after that?" Virginia Woolf lamented in 1922. Well, *To the Lighthouse,* for one, which brings me to my 1955 Harvest Book edition, whose yellow lettering on a blue backdrop above an expanse of blank whiteness makes every other cover of the novel seem either too busy or commonplace. Lighthouses and thoughtful-looking women have adorned the novel's various covers over the years, but none calls to mind the delicious feeling of slowly coursing through the melodic middle part, "Time Passes," which leads to the titular and final section, which begins: "What does it mean then, what can it all mean? Lily Briscoe asked herself, wondering whether, since she had been left alone, it behooved her to go to the kitchen to fetch another cup of coffee or wait here." Could it be that this confluence of an existential and a mundane question is Woolf's answer to Lily's musings? I probably missed this the first time around, but I remember all too well my startled sadness on hearing so casually of Mrs. Ramsay's passing.

I didn't buy many novels when I was young. That's why libraries were invented, and because Dickens's and Dostoevsky's novels were borrowed, I never formed an attachment to their jackets. I did, of course, buy the novels assigned in class, and I came to own a good many more thanks to library sales, but the books that I went out of my way to purchase were those that addressed—well, what Lily wondered about—the meaning of things or, more accurately, how humankind has tried to make sense of the cosmos and our place in it. A tall order and susceptible to philosophical woolgathering, but I was lucky. At twenty-two or -three, I stumbled across my 1971 Cambridge University Press paperback of C. S. Lewis's *The Discarded Image: An Introduction to Medieval and Renaissance Literature* (first published in 1964), which planted in my head the thought that "saving appearances" made the world stay round. I then picked up a second printing of Alexandre Koyré's *From the Closed World to the Infinite Universe* (John Hopkins Press, 1970), which details conceptions of the cosmos from Nicholas of Cusa to Newton. Koyré's is not strictly a scientific work (he was a philosopher and historian of science), whereas my 1953 Dover edition of J. L. E. Dreyer's *A History of Astronomy from Thales to Kepler,* first published by Cambridge University Press in 1906, is definitely more celestial than sublunar.

It's hard to say why I was drawn to these books. I wasn't particularly interested in astronomy, but unanswerable questions about the origins and nature of the universe nibbled away at me. I was intrigued by How it began, but tortured by the Why. Out of Nothing: Something. Out of the imponderable vastness: suddenly heat and gasses and eventually massive grains of matter, and after billions of years, our solar system, and after more billions, life on earth, and then lickety-split in terms of Something, consciousness or Existence as we know it. For what? So we'd learn that we live briefly in an infinitely expanding *and* accelerating universe, a universe with dark matter and dark energy and antimatter and trillions upon trillions of stars, all of which make up a tiny fraction of space—I mean, *what the hell?* "'The stars,' she whispers, 'blindly run,'" Tennyson wrote, scaring me when I was fourteen or fifteen.

I became a teenage cosmologist. I cut out magazine articles whose titles had the words "white dwarfs" or "black holes" in them. I drew my own Ptolemaic map of the cosmos. I kept a notebook about theories of the universe, and even though our galaxy is hurtling through space at over one million miles per hour, I was able to Xerox page after page in books and encyclopedias about the Big Bang. But none of it made any sense—not God, not Creation, not even science. I wanted what the ancients took for granted: the immutability of the heavens.

Unaware, of course, of how pretentious it sounded, I wanted to solve or better yet dissolve the paradox of Existence. Why should Existence even exist? Could it ever have not existed? In most respects, however, I was like any other kid. I hung out with friends, I began to smoke, I played softball, but at night in bed I wondered how the universe came into being and how there could be nothing *but* Existence. Obviously such questions didn't tug at me as I dreamed about Jane or Ann in social studies class, or argued whether Mickey Mantle was better than Ted Williams (he wasn't), but they were certainly the reason I was drawn to philosophy and literature.

Books, I thought, would make sense of things and, at first, poetry, short stories, and novels compensated for the lack of certainty and meaning in life. Then, as I began to read nonfiction, compensation came in the form of the intellectual currents flowing between art, science, literature, and philosophy. E. M. Forster's injunction "Only connect" in *Howard's End* (a fine novel, but not among my 1 percent) not only meant relating to people; it also meant the epiphanic tingle I felt on page 15 in my twelfth printing of Arthur O. Lovejoy's *The Great Chain of Being* (Harvard University Press, 1974): "This change of taste in [English] gardening . . . was the foreshadowing, and one of the joint causes—of a change of taste in all the arts and, indeed, of a change of taste in universes."

The history of ideas has its own publishing history, and during the first half of the twentieth century it nearly became popular history. John Herman Randall, A. N. Whitehead, Norman Cohn, Jacques Barzun, and Isaiah Berlin all wrote books that found their way to my bookshelves, but they came too late to make the same impression as had J. B. Bury's *The Idea of Progress* (1932) and Herbert Butterfield's *The Origins of Modern Science* (1925). Bury's is a 1960 Dover book, and my relationship to Dover Books is an uneasy one. True, the pages are sewn in signatures and the binding won't crack or split, but the absurdly stiff covers give me a pain. Butterfield's book is another story—a smallish paperback (a 1962 "First Collier Books Edition") whose publisher apparently did not believe in margins. Bury informed me of the eighteenth-century quarrel between the Ancients and Moderns (which played such a pivotal role in the development of a literary canon) and notified me that "progress" was an Enlightenment invention. And Butterfield, recounting developments in science, made sure I understood that history has to be interpreted from the point of view of those who generate it and not from the biases and assumptions of the present. These may not seem like theses that quicken the pulse, but to me they put the world in perspective, they provided connections, they yielded order.

Among my bookcases are four of burnished solid oak. Stacked two high, they measure eleven feet across, sixteen inches deep, and eight feet tall and probably hold a good half of my library. Sometimes I gaze at them from across the room and marvel. There's Robert Burton's *The Anatomy of Melancholy* next to Gershom Scholem's *Kabbalah,* and close by is *The Complete Works of Rabelais.* The books don't mock me; I'm very glad I read them, but I can't help thinking that they're mementos of a time when I was less wise and more hopeful, when death had little meaning and the world was ripe with possibilities. And I wonder if holding on to them is the same as holding on to my youth, an endeavor that just may not pan out.

Obviously, I don't know how many of them ended up in my apartment, though I'm pretty sure that my Modern Library editions of Wilde's *De Profundis* (1926) and *Intentions* (undated) were obtained at the biannual library sale held by the Amsterdam branch of the New York Public Library. These small bendy hardcovers, leather bound (or a good imitation), have tenure not only because Wilde was the smartest literary man of his day but also because I had to fight a hundred or so book collectors, including dozens of rude, snarling, ill-dressed book dealers, to get them.

Shoulders and elbows were also necessary to secure my 1922 second edition of *Trivia* by Logan Pearsall Smith, published in 1917 by Doubleday, Page & Company, as well as my 1921 first edition of *More Trivia,* published by Harcourt, Brace, and Company. I hadn't heard of Logan Pearsall Smith (the best name ever for an essayist, though he mainly composed vignettes in "moral prose," some no more than half a page long) until Gore Vidal wrote a piece about him for the *New York Review of Books* in 1984. Smith may not be to everyone's taste, but to me he was the adult in the room: sensible, sensitive, and looking in my mind like Leslie Howard. Well, he didn't as it turns out (Google Images set me straight), but he looks every inch a man of letters, without my knowing, of course, what *that* looks like.

Paging through the essays today, I see that reading him at too young an age is an affectation, while reading him in old age calls into question the slightness of many of the pieces. There may be no happy medium. Here is the entire last entry of *More Trivia;* it's called "The Argument": "This long speculation of life, this thinking and syllogising that always goes on inside me, this running over and over of hypothesis and surmise and supposition—one day this Infinite Argument will have ended, the debate will forever be over, I shall have come to an indisputable conclusion, and my brain will be at rest."

I don't have a clue how I came by my 1974 University of Chicago Press paperback of Frances A. Yates's *The Art of Memory* or her equally magnificent *Giordano Bruno and the Hermetic Tradition,* which I have in the Midway Reprint of 1979, also from Chicago. Nor do I know how to summarize either of these works except to say that Yates was a British historian in the sense that Jussi Björling was a Swedish tenor or Babe Ruth an American baseball player. To my depthless, fidgety mind, Yates's staggering erudition, her comprehensive knowledge of Greek and medieval esoterica, was nothing short of intimidating. Her books made me want to learn all I could about the historical periods she dealt with and, at the same time, suggested that I didn't have the fortitude or the smarts to do them justice.

I may have even paid full price for her books, a rarity, since so many of my books contain a penciled-in figure. My second edition of Joseph Chiari's *Symbolisme from Poe to Mallarmé: The Growth of a Myth* (Gordian Press, 1970, originally published in 1956) set me back, according to the inside cover, $4.50 in August of 1977. The book contains a foreword by Chiari's "great friend"

T. S. Eliot. Chiari, who authored some thirty books, is barely known today, and I probably bought the book *because* of the foreword. Anyway, sitting down with it some forty-five years ago was like catching a movie one had never heard of and being swept up in the story. In this movie, Chiari's introduction and first chapter make up a remarkable document about poetic influence years before W. Jackson Bate and Harold Bloom tackled the subject.

Speaking of Eliot, time may yet dispatch my beat-up 1932 first edition of his *Selected Essays, 1917–1932* (Harcourt, Brace and Company) before I do. Eliot, of course, is the theatrical warhorse of criticism, cited so often that I feel apologetic even mentioning him. But I have no choice. Consulting his essays fifty years ago, I knew I was in the presence of Authority, I felt I was ingesting Authority, and there was something both thrilling and comforting about his pronouncements on the English and French poets. It's terribly unfashionable today to be in thrall to authority, especially to one as "privileged" as Thomas Stearns Eliot, but in 1969 we knew that some writers and artists were just plain better than others. I suppose you could say that I miss the days when writers had dominion over the earth or at least that part of it inhabited by readers who felt that poetry and prose could help explain and sustain their own existence. Can anyone today say of a writer what Maxim Gorky said to himself on first meeting Tolstoy: "I am not an orphan on the earth, so long as this man lives on it"?

Although Chiari's *Symbolisme* covers some of the same ground as Edmund Wilson's *Axel's Castle,* Wilson's book is mentioned only once and only in a footnote. Wilson's first book was the first of his that I read and the first to pique my interest in modern French literature. It was published in 1931, and the pity is that my 1969 paperback edition from Charles Scribner's Sons has a paisley puce-blue-green cover design, which proves I can love what isn't attractive. Wilson wanted to set symbolism in a broader cultural context and uses A. N. Whitehead's *Adventures of Ideas* (my copy is a 1995 Mentor paperback) to demonstrate that just as the Romantic poets had rebelled against the notion "that man was something apart from nature, something introduced into the universe from outside and remaining alien to all that he found," so the symbolist poets disavowed the naturalism and scientific materialism of the mid-nineteenth century. Right, I thought, another example of Camus's nostalgia and one in keeping with Eliot's famous declaration that "in the seventeenth century a dissociation of sensibility set in, from which we have never recovered."

A dissociation that perhaps was never so gallantly expressed as by the French avant-garde around the turn of the twentieth century, and surely no book captured better the forms of this artistic expression than Roger Shattuck's *The Banquet Years,* whose revised 1968 Vintage Books edition jacket encases it like a closet built around one's clothes. John Gerbini designed the cover: a pale blue and two shades of white background hosting the disembodied heads of Erik Satie, Alfred Jarry, Guillaume Apollinaire, and Henri Rousseau. The heads are situated between a flying ten-men tandem bicycle and a vintage photograph of people gathered in a narrow field to watch an early biplane. Maybe it's just me, but I find the cover as indelible, if not as edible, as Proust's *petites madeleines.*

I mention these books not without trepidation. I worry they'll be seen as the "humble brag" of someone who wants the world to know that he has read some pretty highfalutin books. But we can't help what we read when we have no fixed idea about what we plan to do with our lives. These books had my number when the number of my years was relatively few. At fourteen, eighteen, and even twenty-five, certain books light up the mind and affix forever, in case one still isn't sure, one's bookish self. They not only clear the head; they allow you to imagine what others with more imagination have thought and envisioned. And they take your measure: are you really up to *Ulysses*—I mean, do you really **like** *Ulysses*?

The first book I ever bought because I truly wished to own it is a faded red 1915 Oxford edition of *The Poetical Works of John Keats* with gilt lettering that I purchased at Paul's Book Store in Madison, Wisconsin, in 1968. It's a small solid book with gossamery pages whose front matter features a reproduction of Joseph Severn's famous drawing of the poet. Now and then I remove it from a glass-encased bookshelf and hold it in my hands. I believe we have a rapport. I believe we belong together, although I am not by nature a spiritual person. God, destiny, prognostication, and mild forms of paranormal activity do not trouble me. We control what we can until we can't, and if we escape misery or tragedy, it's only because randomness, paradoxically, rules the universe. I say this despite the means by which I acquired a small fraction of my 1 percent.

Thirty years ago I contemplated writing about the British critic and raconteur Desmond MacCarthy. Accordingly, I headed off to Broadway and Thirteenth Street. In those days the literary criticism at the Strand was stuck in with Literature, which was somewhere toward the back of the store, near the left wall. Before I reached the rows designated by the letter M, a book fell from an upper shelf, just missing my head. I knew it was from a high shelf because of the loud clap it made on hitting the floor. It was *Desmond MacCarthy: The Man and His Writings,* a collection of essays put together by the British biographer David Cecil and published in 1984 by Constable and Company Limited. It wasn't the book I was looking for, but what were the chances of this one dropping at my feet, not just in a demure way, but seemingly pushed from a spot it shouldn't have been in the first place at the exact moment I was passing by? This was no random occurrence. The universe and I may not have been reconciled, but at least we were in sync.

But to what purpose? I never did write a piece about MacCarthy, even though I soon found the book I *was* looking for in a used bookstore in Englewood, New Jersey. Titled simply *Criticism,* it was published in 1932 by Putnam and printed in England, and its preface concludes with a nod to Logan Pearsall Smith for help with the selections. Both books were a small revelation. Most critics write as though they know a lot more than their readers, but MacCarthy scribbled or typed as though we all belong to the same bookish fellowship. His prose conveys a modesty that complements rather than distracts from his considerable learning: "When I come across a profound piece of criticism into which the critic has, I feel, been led by surrendering to his own temperament, I wonder if my own method of criticizing is not mistaken." Striving to read impartially, he tamped down his biases and predilections in order to go "straight to the spot where a general panorama of an author's work is visible."

MacCarthy, to my knowledge, never wrote about Kafka, whose temperament was, to put it gently, very different from his own. Kafka had rather high expectations when it came to books. He thought we should "read only the kind of books that wound or stab us . . . that affect us like a disaster, that grieve us deeply, like the death of someone we loved more than ourselves, like being banished into forests far from everyone, like a suicide." Not exactly Dickinson's "Frigate . . . to take us lands away," is it? Kafka's ability to feel the catastrophe in words, I confess, amazes me. Was I ever that sensitive to language? That responsive? Appreciation remains, but disasters . . . disasters are rare.

Then again, I don't buy Emerson's claim that "I cannot remember the books I've read any more than the meals I have eaten; even so, they have made me." Surely the man remembered *some* of the books that made him. Why be coy about it? As for me, my memory isn't a sieve, but it isn't a fortress either. I've got my 1 percent and then some, and when I see the books stacked on

Barzun and Friend

When I was young and thought I knew everything, I met a man who actually did know everything. Or so people said. It was 1970, and I was a first-year graduate student in English and comparative literature at Columbia University. On a whim, I took a crossover seminar offered by the history department that dealt with the writing of history and was taught by Professor Jacques Barzun. Barzun had already published eighteen books, including *The House of Intellect* and *Berlioz and the Romantic Century,* and was famous among students and faculty for his breadth of knowledge. But I hadn't heard of him. I was big for poetry and novels and books that explained the evolution of poetry and novels. I'd also majored in philosophy and took a prideful interest in such arcana as Frances Yates's *Giordano Bruno and the Hermetic Tradition* and E. R. Dodds's *The Greeks and the Irrational.* So Barzun wasn't on my radar, and, for the life of me, I don't know why I signed up for his class.

I showed up to find the only available seat at the end of a long table at whose other end sat a composed, distinguished-looking gent of around sixty. He had neatly combed white hair and what can only be described as a professorial air. "He looked like his name," the psychologist Kenneth Clark observed. "He personified prestige, authority, and self-confidence." No concession was made to the youth culture of the late sixties, when a number of professors began to adopt casual dress and asked to be called by their first names. Barzun looked born in jacket and tie, and from the perspective of an unruly, untutored student used to the unkempt and radical professors I had encountered at the University of Wisconsin, he was something entirely different. Learned, urbane, at ease, he seemed at home both in the academy and at court.

In effect, he seemed a man out of time. Nixon was president, the Vietnam War was going badly, student protests were commonplace, Black ghettos in Newark, Detroit, and Washington, D.C., were kindling for violence, and the Kent State shootings would occur that spring. You could smell pot along upper Broadway, hear the Stones or the Doors blasting from fraternity houses on 114th Street, and revolution was a word that people took seriously. A quick glance would have placed me among them: green army jacket, longish hair, engineer boots, a joint and around a dollar fifty in my pocket. But I had little truck with either radicals or conservatives. I was opposed to the war because I thought it stupid, shameful, and horrific, but politics in general annoyed me. I had books to read, girls to bed, ideas to mull over.

Nor was I a good fit for the academy. I read fiendishly but erratically. I was, to use a cornball phrase, an intellectual loose cannon who took the canon of Great Books on faith. I believed in Shakespeare and Dante, Kafka and Dostoevsky, Proust and Mann; I believed with impregnable certainty that Herrick, Donne, Keats, Yeats, Eliot, and Dylan Thomas were better in an undeniable and absolute sense than other poets. That said, I was also something of an idiot, wasting time playing cards, getting stoned, going to bars and parties, sometimes barely able to get out of bed in the morning.

I mention all this because, for the last forty-two years of his life, Jacques Barzun and I talked on a regular basis. Sometimes we spoke twice a week, sometimes once a month, but it was understood I was not to let too much time pass without getting in touch. When remiss, I'd get a note in the mail informing me of something he'd read or someplace he'd soon be visiting, ending with a question regarding my health or plans—in other words, a gentle reminder to call or write. Less frequently, I'd hear his cultured voice, punctuated by a little throat clearing, on my answering machine, inquiring as to my whereabouts. The obvious question is why Barzun bothered with the likes of me.

I date his curiosity to the second or third class of that winter semester. Although I was the youngest student in the seminar and the only one outside the history department, Barzun paid me no special attention until the subject of Goethe came up (I imagine as a poet deeply interested in history). At some point, one of the students, apparently with Marxist leanings, announced that Goethe had betrayed his genius. What nonsense, I thought. Unfortunately, I also, unintentionally, said it aloud. Barzun looked calmly toward me and asked if I cared to elaborate.

I haven't a notion of what I said fifty years ago or what his response was, but I recall that when I went to his office to discuss the paper I was to write, he engaged me in wide-ranging conversation about my interests, at whose conclusion he pressed on me his 1961 Anchor paperback edition of *Classic, Romantic, and Modern.* When I attempted to return it a week later (thinking foolishly he might actually want it back), he asked me what I thought of it. I said, "It was all right." He laughed.

Truth is, at the time, I thought it no more than a tremendously busy summary of cultural history. It had kept my interest, and I was amazed at the names, books, events, and ideas he threw into the mix, but I was in the grip of Hegel's *Phenomenology of Spirit.* Barzun's book was too light for the twenty-two-year-old intellectual heavyweight I fancied myself to be. And because I had a background in philosophy, I wasn't bowled over by the hot intellectual tickets of the late sixties and seventies, like Barthes, Lacan, and Derrida, who entranced so many American educators. Barzun, too, wasn't enthusiastic about semiotic and deconstructionist readings or about the dogma of indeterminacy, and so we were, on this score, simpatico.

Aside from books, we discussed what was happening around us. Columbia hadn't recovered from the unrest of 1968, when police forcibly removed students from Low Memorial Library, and the campus still had its share of excitable undergraduates ready to protest the war, the companies that supported the war, racial oppression, or governmental policies of various stripes. The film footage of those years had it right: the sixties were for a significant minority another country, which happened to be located in Berkeley, Madison, Manhattan, Cambridge, and on various campuses around the nation. And because I was the right age and enjoyed the perks of drugs, sex, and rock 'n' roll, I suppose I was indistinguishable from most students, even though I didn't quite feel like one of them. For one thing, I left graduate school after a year without a tear of regret from any of my teachers. Even Barzun felt that the field of comparative literature wasn't about to lose an important voice.

He believed, in fact, that the world was going to gain a novelist. I was working on a novel, and he liked that. And when I finished it in the fall of 1971, he asked to see it. I was living at the time with friends in a squalid railroad flat on Avenue B between Sixth and Seventh Streets. A Spanish social hall with pulsing lights bore down on us from across the street, and junkies shambled up and down the block. One morning the phone rang; it was for me. I clambered over naked bodies to pick it up, and I remember thinking, What the hell was Barzun, even the disembodied Barzun, doing on Avenue B? The man sometimes wore an ascot.

I went to see him that very afternoon. His office, on the first floor of Low Library, consisted of a spacious anteroom where sat a receptionist, who guarded the doors at either end. One led to Lionel Trilling's inner sanctum, which I never saw; the other opened into a very large room, where along the right-hand wall sat Barzun's assistant of many years, Virginia Xanthos, who made sure he wasn't bothered by trifles, among which I, at the time, counted myself.

Barzun's was not your typical professor's office. Toward the back of the room, adorned with paintings and covered by a Persian rug, perhaps twenty feet from Virginia, were two comfortable armchairs in front of Barzun's desk, on which that afternoon rested my manuscript "The Death of My Friends" (pretentious is only one word that comes to mind). He thought well of it. He thought so well of it that he had already made a copy and sent it to Simon Michael Bessie, a founder of Atheneum Publishers. He hoped I didn't mind. I assured him I didn't and walked out of Low Library without skipping down the long series of steps that led to street level.

I was not yet twenty-four, and I was going to have a novel published. I don't recall what I did the rest of that day or night. I might have celebrated with friends or perhaps kept the news to myself, delighting secretly in my brilliant future. As it turned out, my future wasn't as bright as I thought. Bessie rejected the novel, making the usual noises about the difficulty of publishing midlist fiction. It was then turned down by the editor-in-chief of Doubleday. And then it was turned down by me. I reread it in light of the editorial comments and realized that the title wasn't the only pretentious thing about it. I tossed it without ceremony into a trashcan along Avenue A.

Now what? I took a job as a night watchman in a rundown hotel on the Upper West Side and worked on short stories. After nine or ten months, I decided to go someplace where I wouldn't get in trouble, where I'd have time to write another novel. A friend recommended Charleston, South Carolina. I called Barzun and told him of my plan, such as it was. He asked me to come by, and when I did, he handed me a check for $800. A gift, he said. I resisted; he insisted. I took it without quite knowing if I should have.

I lived in Charleston on and off for almost a year and wrote another novel, arguably worse than my first. This time Homer didn't nod. Barzun found the book to be the "collegiate" novel I didn't write the first time around. Nonetheless, I submitted it to Alan Williams at Viking Press, one of New York's better-known editors, who thought it showed promise but needed a rewrite. I'm sure he was right, but I wanted to move on and opted against it.

I next found myself in Lexington, Kentucky, driving a truck and submitting short stories to the *New Yorker,* whose fiction editor, Charles (Chip) McGrath, was good enough to return each one with smart, encouraging comments, which led me to keep producing them. I have yet to exact my revenge. Barzun and I exchanged cards and letters, and I think he liked the idea of my hitching around the country, toiling in factories, driving a truck, working construction, while also diligently writing.

I returned to New York in late 1976 and found a small apartment on the Upper West Side. It was a strange time to be in the city. Harlem was drug-ridden and dangerous, and Times Square was about as sleazy as it would ever get. It was pre-AIDS, and the prospect of sex was, if your nose was pointed in the right direction (east, west, north, or south), never far away. Strip joints, topless bars, and S&M clubs were commonplace, and if you were friendly with three or four people around the age of thirty, you'd probably hear about three or four SoHo parties every weekend. Just about everyone I knew smoked pot or did coke and some did H. A night out began around 10 p.m. and might extend to dawn if you knew someone who knew the bartender at an after-hours bar that catered to celebrities, transvestites, and musicians who'd finished their last set.

This was not a New York that Barzun frequented. Nor did he have much to do with the intellectual stirrings around the *Paris Review* or the *New York Review of Books.* He had retired from teaching in 1975 and was now a literary consultant to Charles Scribner's. I'd visit him from time to time in the old Beaux Arts building at 597 Fifth Avenue, and we'd discuss whatever was on my mind and sometimes what was on his. In those days, I was mulling over my fitness as a writer of fiction. Nothing that I wrote seemed worthwhile to me. But I kept at it, and by the end of the decade I had cobbled together a novella about my days as a night watchman, which Barzun urged me to publish. It was oddly touching, the confidence he had in my abilities. Nonetheless, I was reluctant to send the manuscript around because the story seemed forced, and once again I put something aside, keeping only those pages that didn't annoy me. When I told him what I'd done, he called me a "wretch," the first and last time I heard the word applied to anyone.

I didn't feel like a wretch; I felt like someone who was bouncing around the city unsure of what to do next. Then, through a chance encounter, I was offered a job as a part-time semi-editor at Basic Books. Although Barzun was pleased that I was getting a steady paycheck, he was disappointed that I had given up on fiction. Every so often he'd bring up my novella, and I would remind him that I was a wretch and not to expect much. Nonetheless, he remained eager to draw me out on what was happening around town. As usual, he was curious about slang, attitudes, beliefs, goings-on. In telephone calls or during my visits to Scribner's, he'd press me for details about manners and mores, just as he had done in Low Library ten years earlier. I didn't know how many other young people he regularly spoke to, but I liked to think that I was his primary source, reporting on trending events in the culture. Once, on the phone, I wryly remarked to his delight that I was Archie Goodwin to his Nero Wolfe. I knew things he didn't, I went to places he couldn't, I did things he surely wouldn't.

Being young, self-centered, and only a peripheral actor on the cultural scene, I would not fully appreciate the extent of Barzun's interests and activities for several years. It would take too long to list his various positions, but if anyone contradicted the idea of the intellectual who gets his pocket picked while reading Nietzsche, that person was Jacques Barzun. From 1951 to 1963, he, along with Trilling and W. H. Auden, ran the Readers' Subscription Book Club and its successor, the Mid-Century Book Club. From 1955 to 1968, he served as dean of the graduate faculties and then provost of Columbia University. He was a consultant to *Life* magazine, the literary critic for *Harper's* magazine, a director of the Macmillan publishing company, a member of the Council on Foreign Relations, a director of the Council for Basic Education, and twice president of the American Academy of Arts and Letters, all the while serving on numerous boards, including those of the Boston Athenaeum, the Aspen Institute, and the *American Scholar.*

Not to put too fine a point on it, he was more accomplished than the person writing these words. To those few who knew us both, we presented a curious juxtaposition. But it wasn't simply a matter of opposites attracting, although I think we both enjoyed the weak gravitational force between us. Where he was calm, I was quick to anger. Where he exemplified prestige, I eschewed the institutions necessary to attain it. Where I reacted hotly to people and their behavior, he concluded that "resentment is a form of ego I detest." And I believe it was my unsettled state that drew me to him and, in a strange way, him to me. Even a malcontent can come in handy.

One morning he called to tell me that he had been asked to contribute an essay to a journal. He had submitted the article on time but never heard again from the journal's editor, nor had he received the promised honorarium. He wondered if I knew anything about the editor. I replied I did not. "Ah, that's too bad," Barzun said, or words to that effect. He paused. I waited. The penny dropped. "Perhaps I can find out what the problem is," I offered. "Would you?" he said. I would, and I did, and he received a check some weeks later.

"The scruffier the lad the more [Barzun] liked him," Diana Trilling observed without humor. Not sure how scruffy I was in 1970, but I think he enjoyed the company of someone who moved in less rarefied circles. It's awkward and self-serving trying to convey why someone likes or approves of you, but certainly there grew a bond between us that strengthened as the decades passed. And when I began to review books and write critical essays in the early 1980s, he was happy to review my work, which he treated as he did that of any addled student. In his tiny but legible scrawl, he identified every grammatical or factual error, every instance of ambiguity, every word choice he thought slightly off the mark or perhaps too colloquial.

His ministrations aside, I knew my way around books and soon began contributing to half a dozen journals and newspapers. I wasn't getting rich, but I was getting by. Partially to help me along, he asked me in 1988 to edit a collection of essays and addresses that he had lying around. As his editor, I was someone who presumably could improve his work, especially the pieces composed to be read aloud. Barzun, who had already railed in print about the meddling of copy editors, was not—shall we say?—amenable to every suggestion. If he had a flaw as a writer, it was that his credo of "simple and direct" could at times descend into a monotone. Given the extraordinary amount of work he produced, it wasn't a serious failing, but I wanted him to do better whenever possible, and so I rewrote sentences and passages because I knew he wouldn't stand for it. Sure enough, he quickly rewrote me, and we were both happier for it, though only one of us admitted it.

By the time he asked me to put together a collection of the review essays that he, Auden, and Trilling had written for the

Readers' Subscription and Mid-Century book clubs, we had been friends for almost thirty years and worked together amiably, perhaps because I was now, as I told him, getting to be as old as he was. Thankfully, he never did become old in the sense that his mind slowed or he forgot important events. One reason he remained sharp is that his curiosity never flagged. You'd think that his numerous interests and duties would have kept him constantly busy, but give him something that offered a challenge and he'd take it on. When I was subcontracted one year to write capsule arguments and questions for the LSAT, he sent me three of his own invention, which were far too subtle and complicated to use. When I began to write screenplays, he offered to help in writing one about Napoleon in Egypt.

The eighties turned into the nineties, and the world inside and outside the academy changed. Highbrow and lowbrow collapsed in the plastic arts and then in publishing. Identity politics reared its head and its long, spreading body soon followed. In classrooms, the humanities, instead of assessing culture, were now pressured to respond to shifting social attitudes. The intrusion of politics, of right thinking, of carefully weighted words in the teaching of books was not something that Barzun approved of, but he addressed it without rancor. Asked how he would describe himself politically, he replied, "Like any sensible man, I am a liberal, a conservative, and a radical." And then, because he began to devote himself to his longest and most comprehensive book, and because his wife was from Texas, and because New York winters were beginning to get him down, he moved in 1996 to San Antonio.

Face-to-face meetings were now less frequent, but there was the phone and the U.S. mail (he never bothered with email), and we continued to speak of cabbages and kings, of books, music, current events, and people he'd known, an assortment that included Marcel Duchamp, Richard Rodgers, Willy Brandt, Philip

Johnson, Lincoln Kirstein, Colin Davis, William Paley, John Kenneth Galbraith, Herman Wouk, Andy Rooney. And these are only the ones I remember. What did we not talk about? His family, my family, and what caused us grief or pain. He enjoyed conversation, but not where one confided too much. Henry Graff, the presidential historian, who collaborated with Barzun on six editions of *The Modern Researcher,* told me that he could not remember when he and Barzun last talked about "personal stuff." "I consider him a good friend," Graff said. "I talk to him once a week; I've always felt comfortable with him, but I never spent an hour with him the way I did with Trilling, when I'd run into Lionel on the street or in the post office, and we'd stand around and jabber on about everything."

Quite so. Barzun didn't jabber. It's not that he was concealing Baron de Charlus–like tendencies (as alluring as that thought is); he simply felt you shouldn't be interested in his personal life because, after all, what did it have to do with you? And what did it have to do with his work? Formality was in order. Formality, he maintained, fostered clear thinking, whereas casualness tended to break down the natural barriers between people, leading to indifference and perhaps contempt. For Barzun, a noisy bonhomie, forced egalitarianism, and unwanted advances chipped away at one's sense of self. Therefore, manners, by protecting the self, were a civilizing influence, not merely a by-product of the class system.

In fact, it was his imperturbability that appealed, his being content to keep our relationship at a slight remove. I, too, didn't want to get closer; I didn't want him all of a sudden to open up his arms, enfold me in his personal fears and disappointments, and tell me how he felt about the loss of his second wife or the problems he had with his children or the spitting hatreds coiling inside him. I didn't want to be on an equal footing, not because he was forty years older but because he was the adult whose intellect and experience conferred prestige on his opinion of me. Hell, for years I didn't want to call him by his first name because it felt wrong. He was the significant teacher I'd never had before, not necessarily the one who knew more than I did (which, of course, he did), but the one who seemed to have mastered his role in the world. I liked it that he could deftly and somehow impersonally move through life while I, in my twenties and thirties, careened into and off friendships and relationships. And no matter what happened, he was there, not to do anything so unoriginal as "support" me but simply to represent continuity and order. He was a constant; he never changed. He grew old and frail. His hearing grew worse, he developed tremors in his hand, he broke a hip. But his mind—until the last week of his life—remained the mind that I had first encountered in 1970.

Over the years I ran into academics who thought he had spread himself too thin, who dismissed him for his own dismissal of intellectual trends, or who found his conservative views obsolescent. It didn't bother him. He had been born in France at the beginning of the twentieth century and witnessed two world wars. His temperament leaned toward the classical, but his intellect, formed when modernism and surrealism were getting under way, stayed open to ideas and innovation in the arts. Very little surprised or impressed him, but he reserved his cynicism for those artists or intellectuals who thought well of themselves without properly understanding how unoriginal they were. Conduct, he believed, affected character, and "a person's character is known by the concepts he keeps." I can't name too many thinkers who would say that. Kant, perhaps? Or maybe a moral philosopher like G. E. Moore?

In any event, Barzun did say it and followed up by subscribing to William James's notion that every reasonable request incurs a moral obligation in the person petitioned, and that granting such requests helps "'moralize' the universe." And, as many writers can attest, Barzun was a soft touch: he'd read supplicants' manuscripts even if they were five hundred pages long. For years I tried to get him to cut back, but he acceded only when he turned ninety-nine or thereabouts. How he managed to produce so many books, while carrying out his teaching and administrative duties, is beyond me. Despite all this, I was surprised when an English professor of my acquaintance referred to him as "a great man."

Was he a great man? It never occurred to me to wonder. What constitutes greatness in a person—specifically someone who deals in ideas? Books and reputation are not enough. Although Barzun received the Presidential Medal of Freedom in 2003 and seven years later the National Humanities Medal, he would have been the first to pooh-pooh such honors. In fact, he declined all honorary degrees and refused to accept awards that had money attached. It was the work that mattered, not the acclaim that might or might not accrue. And his work, aside from teaching, was examining music, opera, history, etymology, Romanticism, French verse, American education, science, baseball, detective fiction, Montaigne, Rousseau, Diderot, Darwin, Wagner, Berlioz, Liszt, Abraham Lincoln, John Jay Chapman, William James, et al.

He had, of course, read all the historians from Herodotus to Hofstadter, but what sometimes gets underplayed is that he was a cultural historian. The term gets tossed around (less these days than formerly), but I'm not sure we ever understood it as Barzun did. Basically, he felt that he had to acquaint himself with everything that contributed to both the fact and the theory of civilization. It all interested him because it was all related. "The essence of culture," he wrote, "is interpenetration. From any part of it the searching eye will discover connections with another part seemingly remote." For Barzun, this meant synthesizing huge amounts of information in fields beyond the purview of historians proper. How many scholars could discuss music with Arturo Toscanini, architecture with Daniel Libeskind, and fictional sleuthing with Rex Stout? Who but Barzun would have deduced that Bernard Shaw read French newspapers because in one of his plays he mentions a crime that had been reported only in the French press?

Barzun didn't just study history, he considered everything that man had achieved or tried to achieve from the Renaissance onward, and what he considered, he remembered. His magnum opus, *From Dawn to Decadence,* published in 2000 when he was ninety-two, contains an index that lists every man or woman who contributed something lasting to Western culture over the past five hundred years. A surprising best seller, it's also a book that the British commentator Alistair Cooke proclaimed "may fairly take its place alongside Gibbon," which is a little like seating a contemporary playwright alongside Shakespeare.

What strikes me, however, is not the usual encomiums but the unusual concurrence of opinion about much of Barzun's work. He was a darling of conservative critics like Hilton Kramer, Roger Kimball, and William Safire, yet he did not lack for more liberal-leaning admirers such as Anne Fadiman, Michael Dirda, and Morris Dickstein. I attribute this to a mind fully aware of its debt to other minds which then serenely strikes out on its own. For better or worse, Barzun was sometimes a middlebrow popularizer (*Science: The Glorious Entertainment*), a guide to fledgling scholars (*The Modern Researcher*), a teacher of history who condemned its corruption by the academy (*Clio and the Doctors*), a composer of clerihews and satires under the name of Roger du Béarn, a musicologist (*Music in American Life*), an educator (*Teacher in America; The House of Intellect*), a psychologist/philosopher (*A Stroll with William James*), and finally the man who knew everything (*Berlioz and the Romantic Century*).

He had his disagreements with historians and writers (Leon Edel, for one, regarding something William James wrote), but I never came across a true vilifier except for Evelyn Waugh. In the winter of 1951, *Life* magazine sent Barzun to interview the novelist. Afterward, Waugh decided that Barzun had scotched his deal with the magazine: "*Life* had sent a smart-aleck down here," he wrote to Graham Greene, "and that has ended my profitable connextion with them" (Feb. 27, 1952). Waugh's diary entry reiterates the sentiment: "They sent me an apostate frog called professor Smart-Aleck Baboon. He stayed here and gave me a viva in history and reported all." Which makes me wonder if Waugh's pen was dipped in imperceptible acid when he wrote, "Dear Professor, I enjoyed our conversation so much last night. Do come again" (Dec. 18, 1951).

Like anyone else, he was fallible—just less so. He was not above pique and not above rushing to judgment. When someone misled him about my own conduct, he wrote to me in reproof but apologized immediately when informed of the truth. How he conducted himself in private or with his family is something I know little about. I know he had a temper; I also know that he was not as self-contained as he wanted people to think. And I know that he was drawn to powerful emotions and believed them to be the bedrock of great music and literature. Although I'm certain that he would be able to reconcile his advocacy of manners with his preference for visceral works of art, I doubt that I would buy his explanation. People are complicated, and some people are more complicated than others.

We didn't always see eye to eye. For one thing, he ruled out the idea that any one period could sum up either the best or the worst that humans are capable of. I don't know that I agreed with him. From where I sit, the twentieth century was terrible in a way that other centuries were not, if only because history had shown us the horrors of dictatorships and mechanized war and still we allowed the rise of Hitler and Stalin and Mao. As I listened to him expatiate on inventions, revolutions, and the unpredictable course of history, I recognized that his was always the long view. But how to determine whether equanimity in the face of discordant change is a result of learning or of temperament? In the end, it doesn't matter. Because when attending closely to someone else's view of the world, one sees that the degree and kind of knowledge derived from experience depends on age, health, biases, and inclinations, and on what one is willing to do to acquire it.

This may seem too bald a statement to have merit, but often it's the differences between us, when examined intelligently and assimilated imaginatively, that produce something approaching wisdom. Not that this insight figured significantly in my own life, but I believe it characterized Barzun's approach to things. He took the time to examine his relation to the world, which meant putting some distance between himself and others, and because of the way he carried himself, it took me a while to understand that he was able to care for me because it was safe to care. He could invest emotion in me because the risk wasn't great; it didn't interfere with his work. When I told his son-in-law that Barzun had hugged me before he went off to San Antonio, he expressed surprise, and I realized that Barzun was not demonstrative with his own children. Am I making excuses for him in hazarding that the cost would have been too great, that he was far too busy teaching, writing, and being in the world to expend the emotion desired by those closest to him, those who depended on him? Because he sensed I was not dependent, no matter my affection, he allowed himself to show affection for me.

And Barzun was safe for me, too. As an only child whose mother died early, I grew up with an overly protective father who was so emotionally involved in my well-being that I left home as soon as I could. Convinced that my writing would lead nowhere, he worried about me incessantly and for twenty years tried to dissuade me from the writing life. So it doesn't take a psychologist to know why Barzun was a welcome alternative. His reserve, his steadiness, his belief in me obviated any potential explosiveness of the kind that existed in my other filial relationship.

More important, he had a soothing effect on me. I was calmer in his presence, as if the world wasn't all about struggle, competition, and jockeying for position. Somehow he seemed detached from such things, and it was a detachment that subtly transferred to me. And when I think back on how little I knew then and how well I thought of myself (the two obviously went hand in hand), I see that he came along at a moment when I needed someone who represented what adulthood could be like, even if I sensed that my own would be very different. And so, for forty years, whenever I heard his distinct but slightly throaty voice, the world made a little bit more sense, and it was a pleasure to make him laugh.

The last time I saw him was in 2007 in San Antonio. I was doing a piece about him for the *New Yorker* on the occasion of his hundredth birthday. One afternoon, he said something that elicited a chuckle from me. He looked over and said casually, "You can include that when you write about me." He meant down the road sometime. Unthinkingly, I replied, "Oh, I think this will be it." He looked more puzzled than hurt, and I have always regretted brushing aside his suggestion. I knew why I had done so. I had already edited two books with his name on them and I didn't want my own name to be automatically linked to his. Enough people knew of our friendship, and someone had even suggested that I was his Boswell. I wasn't; he has an official biographer, and frankly I wanted to ward off such perceptions. I was his friend, not an acolyte or protégé. It was this disinclination that made me palatable to him. At any rate, I wished many times that I had not demurred so quickly. What the hell do we know about how we're going to feel tomorrow?

In my case, there was grief. Then emptiness. Then, after a few years, more emptiness. Emptiness is the right word even though it's a misnomer. How can there be emptiness when there is thought and emotion? Not a fine distinction, but one I might have mentioned to the man whose absence is the cause of the emptiness. Jacques died on October 25, 2012, five weeks shy of his 105th birthday.

Originally published in the *American Scholar,* Spring 2021.

What's the Deal, Hummingbird?

A STORY

On or around May 5th of 2020, he just stopped. He stopped exercising, stopped walking, stopped reading, stopped planning. He ate, drank, washed, and paid the bills, but that was it. He was seventy-three. He'd spent more than 38,368,800 minutes on earth, only a precious few of which he remembered. That's what hit him one evening, after the cheering and clanking of pots and pans had died down: a vast chunk of his life—the greater part of his life—might as well never have occurred. Not just the time spent sleeping but those millions of minutes spanning lunches, dinners, meetings, concerts, marriage, work, books, movies, conversations—all gone. What remained? A bird's breath of his existence. Sitting with his mother in Prospect Park when an actual bird had shat on her dress and he, eight years old, thought the world had swerved off course. Wounding a squirrel with a BB gun when he was ten and crying over the small quivering body. Losing a footrace when he was twelve because he was so far ahead he thought he could slow down. Sparring at seventeen with a handsome Black kid who fought as an amateur under the name of Voodoo DaLeeba. Smoking a joint in Sheridan Square Park when an old man in tattered clothes approached and said, "If you tell me you love me, I'll tell you how to make a lot of money." Watching *2001: A Space Odyssey* in a movie theater on Fifty-First Street and softly whistling when the dark bone flung into the air descends and suddenly there's a white satellite sailing through space. Running headlong down a steep hill in a Kentucky hollow, exhilarated by the danger of falling and breaking his legs. Bumping into a friend, who told him that she had slept with two men that day, and it so aroused him that he asked if he could be the third. Inhaling an intensely aromatic 1990 La Tâche at a Sotheby's pre-auction tasting. Listening as Seiji Ozawa conducted *The Rite of Spring* at Tanglewood when the skies darkened and thunder rumbled and a hard slanting rain gusted into the shed, spraying the audience and the musicians onstage. Ozawa didn't seem to notice, but *he* noticed that the musicians were smiling, almost grimacing. The strings cried with the wind and thumped with the drums, and the horns played searing notes in various keys and it was so goddamn wonderful that he never even thought to look over at his girlfriend.

For a time, he wanted to live for art, a fatuous notion since he couldn't write, paint, or sculpt, and played the piano with a vague melancholic air that impressed no one. A small trust allowed him some leeway during the seventies, but once he had his fill of moving around he took a job in a large advertising agency where he made nice with people he often liked but never admired. When he was thirty, he met a woman whose skin and smell were so intoxicating that he foolishly spent every dollar he earned trying to hold on to her, even though he knew it was hopeless. She was twenty-four and thought cocaine, vodka gimlets, and going to CBGB part of the natural life cycle. Five months after she totaled her dark-blue MG, killing herself and a grad student, he married someone who knew more about books than he did. She didn't want children and, after a while, he didn't either. His wife was a writer and a lecturer at various colleges, mostly in the East, so he met a lot of people in the arts, all but one of whom disappeared from his life after the divorce. How many times had he slept with his wife in nineteen years of marriage and the four months before that? Nineteen hundred times? Three thousand times? Five thousand four hundred and twenty-two? Shouldn't he remember how it felt at least some of those days and nights? It's so damned intimate being inside another person. Isn't it?

In the morning, he occasionally listened to Ben Webster.

By August 2020 his sense of time had gone kablooey. Events thirty years in the distance now knocked at the door, while things he'd done five weeks earlier seemed impossibly remote. He remembered watching war movies made in 1945 and thinking they were ancient because it was 1960. Now he thought *The Graduate* and *Jaws* were contemporary films. How do you know what you've forgotten? He knew only that he was a case of nerves between two eternities. His first day of college—that he remembered. He'd stood in line to register behind a tall, light-haired, long-legged girl who ended up in two of his classes. It was 1965 and she came to class barefoot, wearing skimpy white shorts. He remembered one of their professors saying, "As long as you're alive, you're immortal." He believed that for about five minutes and then he wondered how many other professors got things wrong. He remembered getting drunk and wanting to fight a cop during a protest against Dow Chemical, and being pulled away by his roommate. He remembered a long purple-and-white scarf he wore in college that no one else remembered. He remembered sitting in the Jardin des Tuileries next to a handsome middle-aged woman and her daughter, who looked like Catherine Deneuve. They struck up a conversation and the woman invited him to lunch, but he declined. Why? He remembered going into a pâtisserie after having rehearsed saying "Je voudrais acheter une boîte de chocolats" and being mistaken for a Parisian. He remembered a sunset in Provence, a hostel in Montpellier where he played Ping-Pong, a dog he almost hit when he was driving from Nice to Antibes. He remembered his wife pressing him to read *The Death of*

Ivan Ilyich. He read it and was bored. He remembered dropping acid on Martha's Vineyard and asking everyone who Martha was. No one knew. He remembered the last woman he had slept with. She had been sixty-two. How strange was that? He remembered the first time he removed a girl's bra, only to think about a character in *Catch-22* who claimed that life is all downhill after that. He remembered meeting Joseph Heller at the office of the Brooklyn parks commissioner back in 1998 or '99. He remembered being face to bosom with Jackie Onassis as he was going up the stairs at the Metropolitan Opera and she was coming down. He remembered sitting on the Sixty-Fifth Street crosstown bus opposite Paul Newman, who was wearing a beautiful tan shearling coat and orange-tinted sunglasses. He remembered Lauren Bacall, leaning on a walker, asking him to reach for something on a shelf at Zabar's. He remembered sitting in a Thai restaurant at a table next to Mick Jagger, Jerry Hall, and two bodyguards. Jagger caught him sneaking a glance and said, "It makes the food taste better, don't it?" He remembered sitting across from John Updike on a 1 train heading downtown from 155th Street. He remembered getting into an argument with Christopher Hitchens over who disliked Henry Kissinger more. He remembered shaking the hand of Willie Pep in a high school gym in West Orange, New Jersey. Pep was old by then and his small hand was soft and felt padded.

In the morning, he sometimes listened to the *Pastoral* Symphony.

Even before the pandemic, he barely heard from anyone. His old college friends were more absorbed than ever in the lives of their children and grandchildren, and he had neither one nor the other. "Social media" were words he heard a lot but they meant nothing to him. He didn't have many close friends. One had died of a stroke; another had killed himself by jumping from a ferry in the English Channel, his body never recovered. When he looked at people he knew, he considered their absence. He himself was more or less in good health: no blood-pressure pills, no blood thinners, no prostate issues. But he had no energy. Without anyone cooking for him or watching what he ate, he subsisted on sandwiches, takeout, and Entenmann's. With nothing to do, he began thinking about suicide. But suicide required planning and he wasn't up to it. He owned a gun, but he wasn't about to shoot himself or leap to his death or jump in front of a train, and pills were not foolproof. Then the pandemic hit and he stopped thinking about dying.

The pandemic perked him up. He didn't tell people that, but, come on, it was the most interesting thing to happen to the world since 9/11. He didn't downplay the misery and suffering it caused, but that was the point: it killed people. Every day there was a body count, every day there were stories of loss, separation, and grief. Every day he read about or heard accounts of the heroic behavior of essential workers, frontline workers, and first responders, of spouses and children keeping vigil outside hospitals that shut them out. Life had become a constant threat to life. It was a goddamn ticking time bomb is what it was. Sure, it could feel good when you were young and fit, but what had he done with his youth? He had never kept a diary and regretted, even resented, not knowing where he'd been or what he'd felt at 12:48 p.m. on November 2, 1978. It wasn't supposed to be this way. He'd retired when he was sixty-nine, but he'd still gone through the motions. He went out, attended openings and the opera, dined in good restaurants, borrowed books from the Society Library, and visited New Orleans and San Francisco. He even tried snorkeling in the Keys. But COVID put a stop to that, and then he stopped.

Obviously, he was afraid of catching the virus, but he rather liked the masks, the forced anonymity, the social distancing, the sense of fear on the streets. He didn't mind lining up to get into a CVS and he got used to ordering his groceries over the phone, though the stores always got something wrong. And though he no longer walked regularly, he'd go out after it rained, when there were fewer people around. He now had an excuse for doing what he always wanted to do: live in the world without anyone noticing. Instead of feeling housebound, he felt content to be at home. And now when he had nothing to do, he felt justified in doing nothing. As for boredom, well, sure, but when had he ever not been bored?

"You need to get Netflix," his ex-wife told him. She had called him about two weeks after New York went into lockdown, partly out of guilt and partly because she was just a nice person. "Watch *Call My Agent,*" she said. "It'll cheer you up." He promised her he would, without intending to follow through, but she knew him, so she put him on her account and emailed him her password, which obligated him to watch it. She was right: it cheered him up. He asked her what else he should watch and quickly marshaled against the plague—as though they were chess pieces in his match with boredom—*Longmire, Get Shorty, Sneaky Pete, Justified, Line of Duty, The Kominsky Method, Peaky Blinders, Ozark, Bosch, The Americans, A French Village, The Queen's Gambit,* and the always soothing *The Durrells in Corfu.* Damn it if he didn't begin to live with these imaginary people, and he hated it when a series ended. It was like the death of a friend, several friends. What he needed, he told his ex, was a series that would run for as long as he did.

"Give *Cobra Kai* a try," she emailed one night.

"No, there are limits," he wrote back.

"Do it," she said.

One night, six months into the pandemic, when no one knew how bad it would get, he watched *The Third Man,* which he hadn't seen in thirty years, and partway through, as he lay on his couch, he began to feel something he had trouble identifying. It took a few seconds to understand that he felt happy. The writing, the direction, the acting, the lighting, the set design, the music, the cinematography—everything worked so well that he wanted to call up Graham Greene and ask him, What's the deal with the stupid, annoying landlady? Why couldn't he have left her out?

Sometimes in the afternoon he listened to Al Green or Sam Cooke or the Staple Singers.

Music had always been there. He had grown up listening to the radio, to Cousin Brucie, Murray the K, and, later, switching over to FM, Jonathan Schwartz and Allison Steele. Although he didn't remember the first time he heard the Shirelles singing "Will You Still Love Me Tomorrow?," it was the first popular song that had stuck with him. He remembered the first time he heard "Satisfaction," the first time he heard a recording of Bill Evans playing "Some Other Time," the first time he heard the Toccata and Fugue in D Minor on WQXR, the station of the *New York Times.* He remembered George Jellinek, but not the other hosts. He remembered Lenny Bernstein saying, in some interview or other, that he found it hard to breathe when conducting the *Missa Solemnis.* If he had to guess, it would be during the Sanctus, about fifty-three minutes into the piece and lasting a little under thirteen minutes. Pensive strings with light support from flutes usher in a radiant violin solo right before the Benedictus. Only Beethoven could have written this, and hearing it made the world bearable for a while.

Music cut out the noise. Rock, country, folk, jazz, or classical, it didn't matter; it cut out the noise. And, Lord knows, there was plenty of noise now. The nation seemed to be imploding. Watching the news, switching between Fox and CNN, he remembered a movie he'd seen some years back; it could have been five, it could have been ten. The movie was available on demand, so he watched it again and liked it, but thought it sometimes talked because it could. Brad Pitt played a hit man who shows up at a bar to get paid off. But the man who hired him now feels he deserves a discount. They discuss it while a small TV overlooking the bar plays a live feed of a youngish Barack Obama delivering his election victory speech. When he gets to the part about America being one country, one community—out of many, one—Pitt's character scoffs, "It's a myth created by Thomas Jefferson . . . a rich wine snob who was sick of paying taxes to the Brits." Pitt's hard-bitten cynicism caps the film. "Don't make me laugh," he says. "I'm living in America, and in America, you're on your own. America's not a country. It's just a business. Now fucking pay me."

He had never given much thought to what America was about. It was above his pay grade. Once, it had been about the old versus the young, about supporting the war in Vietnam or opposing it, but, with the televised killing of George Floyd, America had become a misfire, a moral mare's nest. We'd found the secret portrait recording our sins: slavery, Jim Crow, our treatment of Chinese workers, Native Americans, unions, women. But it was still America, right? Give me liberty or give me death. Four score and seven years ago. Ask not what your country can do for you. "When the values go up up up / And the prices go down down down / Robert Hall this season / Will show you the reason / Low overhead." Compared to murdering fucking Nazis and crazed, robotic Japanese soldiers, we were goddamn saints. Anyway, what was he supposed to do about it? His skin puckered on the inside of his elbows, hair grew in his ears, dark spots mottled the backs of his hands—what do you call them? Liver spots, sun spots, age spots? Too many to know which were recent and which had been around a while. He should have taken pictures of them and dated each photo, so he could track their number and location, a chronological map that led to oblivion. In the meantime, noise.

in a cage in the Bronx Zoo. The cage was small and filthy and sat on wheels. He remembered the first time he had crunched into butterfly shrimp in a Chinese restaurant. He remembered that he had remembered and then forgotten the name of the duck dish that he used to order in a restaurant that had long since closed. He remembered frankfurters sizzling on a grill at a deli called Schweller's. He remembered a game of touch football in Brookline, or was it Boston? He remembered a pipe he had smoked for a year after quitting cigarettes. He remembered a pair of Frye boots that he had worn to the ground. He remembered jogging around the Central Park Reservoir a few yards behind Willie Nelson. He remembered a lyric about listening to Chet Baker on the beach, in the sand, with the leaves falling down. He remembered a hysterical woman in a bloody nightgown stopping him on West End Avenue brandishing a carving knife. It was late, the street was deserted, and the woman was screaming in Spanish. He calmed her down and cautiously pried the knife from her fingers, which is how the police, guns in hand, found them: a twenty-something man holding a large knife, and a woman in a nightgown covered in blood. He remembered a piece of pineapple upside-down cake a girlfriend's mother had given him. He remembered hitching from Paris to Calais one summer and getting picked up in a cream-colored Rolls-Royce by a London publisher, who took him home and played him recordings of Schubert's lieder. He remembered being driven off the highway outside Covington, Kentucky, by a man who wanted to have sex with him. He remembered the Lionel electric train set that his father had bought him after his mother died. He remembered the afternoon that his mother, wearing a green velour hat, had picked him up at day care. Upon seeing her, he had exclaimed, "What's the deal, hummingbird?," and she had given him a brilliant smile and replied, "Hey, what's the word, banana peel?" For the whole ride back to the house, she had chuckled and tousled his hair, and when they got home she picked up the phone and called his father. She then motioned him over so he could speak into the receiver. He repeated what he'd said and his father slowly let out his deep-chested laugh. "So what's the word, banana peel?" he roared.

Why, isn't that enough for a whole lifetime?

Originally published in the *New Yorker,* January 17, 2022.

ACKNOWLEDGMENTS

The author would like to thank:

Henry Finder and Deborah Treisman at the *New Yorker.*
Robert Wilson and Sudip Bose at the *American Scholar.*
Jackson Lears and Stephanie Volmer at *Raritan.*
Boris Dralyuk at the *Los Angeles Review of Books.*

At the University of Virginia Press, Eric Brandt accommodated my disposition as well as my prose with barely a shudder, and Ellen Satrom was extremely helpful in correcting, refining, and improving the latter.

Dasha Kiper remains my best reader. She knows when I write too much, but more importantly, when I say too little. Without her wise counsel, many of these essays would be much the poorer.